POPULATION GROWTH

POPULATION GROWTH

By

Dr. M. LAKSHMI NARASAIAH

M.A., Ph.D.

Professor and Head

Department of Economics

Sri Krishnadevaraya University Post-Graduate Centre

Kurnool-518 002 (A.P.)

DISCOVERY PUBLISHING HOUSE

NEW DELHI-110 002

First Published-2001

Reprinted-2011

ISBN 81-7141-584-9

Published by
DISCOVERY PUBLISHING HOUSE
4831/24, Ansari Road, Prahlad Street,
Darya Ganj, New Delhi-110002 (India)
Phone: 3279245 • Fax: 91-11-3253475

Printed at:
Mehra Offset Press
Delhi

Preface

During the last half-century world population has more than doubled, climbing from 2.5 billion in 1950 to 5.9 billion in 1998. Those of us born before 1950 are members of the first generation to witness a doubling of world population. Stated otherwise, there has been more growth in population since 1950 than during the 4 million years since our early ancestors first stood upright.

This unprecedented surge in population combined with rising individual consumption, is pushing our claims on the planet beyond its natural limits. Water tables area falling on every continent as demand exceeds the sustainable yield of aquifers. Eventual aquifer depletion will bring irrigation cutbacks and shrinking harvests. Our growing appetite for seafood has pushed oceanic fisheries to their limits and beyond. Collapsing fisheries tell us we can go no further. The Earth's temperature is rising, promising changes in climate that we cannot even anticipate. We are triggering the greatest extinction of plant and animal species since the dinosaurs disappeared. As our numbers go up, their numbers go down.

These effects of population growth are relatively recent, but assertions that population growth could affect human welfare are not. In 1798 Thomas Malthus, a British clergyman and intellectual, warned in his famous piece, *An Essay on the Principles of Population*, of the tendency for population to grow exponentially while food supply grew arithmetically. He saw a world where human numbers would continually press against available food supplies.

During the 200 years since Malthus issued his warning, famine has visited countries as diverse as Ireland and India, Ethiopia and China. Indeed, despite the near-tripling of the world grain harvest since 1950 the hungry and malnourished in 1998 number an estimated 840 million-nearly as many people as lived in the world when Malthus penned his essay.

But the nature of famine has changed. Whereas it was once geographically defined by areas of poor harvests, today famine is economically defined by low incomes in those segments of society that lack the purchasing power to buy enough food. Famine concentrated among the poor is less visible than the more traditional version but is no less real.

In addition to checks imposed by food shortages, there is evidence that other checks on population growth are now emerging, such as new infectious diseases, including AIDS, Ethnic conflicts within societies, such as Rwanada and the Sudan, are also taking a growing toll. Water shortages on a scale that would deprive people of enough water to produce food could undermine governments.

The evidence gathered here indicates that the rapid population growth prevailing in a majority of the world's countries is not going to continue much longer. Either countries will get their act together,. shifting quickly to smaller families, or death rates will rise from one or more of the stresses just mentioned. As human demands press against more and more of the Earth's limits, the questions is not whether population growth will slow, but how. Will it be because countries do it humanely by shifting quickly to smaller families? Or because they fail to do so, and nature ruthlessly imposes its own constraints? In a world facing many challenges as it prepares to enter the next century, this may be the most challenging of all.

Author

Contents

1

Welcome, Baby Six Billion

Somewhere, sometime, we will be able to welcome the six billionth human being on earth. Nobody knows exactly, when this figure will be reached, since census data are sketchy and unreliable in many parts of the world. So it's nothing more than a projection, but an interesting figure nevertheless. In July 1987, the United Nations had officially greeted the arrival of the five billionth citizen to our world. At that time, UN estimates were that by the year 2000, world population would stand at about 6.25 billion people. Reality has proven to be more favourable than that prognosis: population growth has slowed down considerably during the last decade. The growth rate is now 1.33 per cent or 78 million people per year, and although figures will continue to go up at least during the first half of the next century, the point of stabilization may be reached earlier than expected. Latest UN projections for the year 2050 speak of 8.0 billion people instead of the 9.8 billion predicted in 1994.

The reasons for the success achieved in slowing population growth lie in the importance attached to family planning and reproductive health by governments and NGOs in developing countries as well as the general advances made. In education, health services, and the emancipation of women. It is remarkable now quickly fertility—the average number of children born by each woman—has fallen in most countries. In more than 60 countries, the fertility rate is now 2.1 children per woman or below—which means that the population in those countries is stagnant or even getting smaller. World average is now 2.7 children per woman; even in Africa, fertility has fallen from 6.6 to 5.1 children per woman within a quarter of a century. The majority of women now want to limit the number of children to be able to bring them up better, and more couples than ever have the means and knowledge to control their family size. The world population conference in Cairo in 1994 gave a further push for population policies which aim at sustainable development and a balance between population figures and resources.

However, these positive developments should not be a cause for exaggerated self-gratulations. Not all is well after Cairo; in fact, most of the rich industrial states who pledged to generously support the developing countries in the Cairo Plan of Action are in no way living up to their obligations. Instead of 5.7 billion dollars in international aid, only 1.4 billion annually are actually forthcoming. Development aid from OECD countries has fallen significantly since 1994. Only the Scandinavian countries and the Netherlands—the usual suspects— are paying their share of the costs. Germany also met its commitments undertaken in Cairo of providing DM 450 million per annum for reproductive health in its bilateral and multilateral development budget. Lack of funds could jeopardise the efforts of Third World governments to provide adequate family planning and health services to their population. This may lead to setbacks in achieving the goals of the Cairo conference. This summer, the UN will hold Special Session of the General Assembly to review 'Cairo +5' to discuss possible action to give new momentum to the Cairo process. But although developing countries are shouldering two-thirds of the burden for population-related activities—7.5 billion dollars per year — this is clearly not sufficient to meet the demand.

Other clouds overshadow the positive balance of this decade. The financial and economic crises in Southeast Asia, Latin America and Eastern Europe led to serious disruptions of social services in the affected countries. Poverty is rising again at dramatic speed in countries like Indonesia or Thailand which had made spectacular advances in population control during the decades of economic boom. If poverty and the lack of health and education services are linked to high fertility levels—as many population scientists believe—the fallout from the crises could result in a reversal for population successes.

A threat of a different nature is looming large over parts of Africa, Asia and Latin America: the effect of the AIDS epidemic on demographic development. At least 40 million people worldwide are infected with HIV, and many of them will die of the deadly disease within the next ten years. HIV-infected people are mostly young and economically active persons, and their illness and possible death will change the demographic parameters. More than 1 billion people worldwide are in the critical age group between 15 and 24 in which half of all HIV cases occur, but many of them are not reached by information about AIDS prevention, and social and sexual habits, social disruptions through wars or migration, and poverty levels make it more difficult than in industrial countries to get the epidemic under control. Already now, life expectancy is falling drastically in parts of the world.

For all these reasons, the future development of world population is difficult to predict. This should not stop us from welcoming 'Baby Six Billion' among our midst. The birth of a new human being should always be a cause of joy and not of fear. The world is large enough and its resources sufficient—if sensibly managed and shared among all people- to allow a life in dignity and free form deprivation for all of us. After all, the much discussed 'carrying capacity' of the world is a relative notion, depending entirely on the kind of lifestyle we adopt for ourselves. Human ingenuity is capable of finding suitable ways to protect our life-sustaining resources such as water, soil, and air. We just have to muster the political will to apply our knowledge and finances to this goal.

Six billion people are, therefore, not a threat to our survival—provided we all change our development models and aspire not to waste and over-consumption but to true sustainabiliy.

2

Population Growth and Jobs

Since mid-century, the world's labour force has more than doubled—from 1.2 billion people to 2.7 billion, outstripping the growth in job creation. As a result, the United Nations International Labour Organization estimates that nearly 1 billion people, approximately 30 per cent of the global work force, are unemployed or underemployed (working but not earning enough to meet basic needs). Over the next half-century, the world will need to create more than 1.9 billion jobs—all of them in the developing world—just to maintain current levels of employment.

As economists often note, while population growth may boost labour demand (through economic activity and demand for goods), it will most definitely boost labour supply. During the next 50 years, almost 40 million people will enter the global labour force—defined as those between the ages of 15 and 65 seeking work—each year. Between 1995 and 2050, some 1.9 billion additional jobs will need to be created to absorb these new would-be workers. The most pressing needs will be found in the world's poorest nations- a sobering example of the vicious cycle linking poverty and population growth.

As the children of today represent the workers of tomorrow, the interaction between population growth and jobs is most acute in nations with young populations. Nations such as Peru, Mexico, Indonesia, and Zambia with more than half their population below the age of 25 will feel the burden of this labour flood. In the Middle East and Africa, 40 per cent of the population is under the age of 15. Since new entrants into the labour force were born at least 15 years ago, measures to reduce population growth have a delayed affect on the growth of the labour force, highlighting the urgency of taking action on population.

Nowhere is the employment challenge greater than in Africa, where at least 40 per cent of the population lives in absolute poverty. Although 8 million people entered the sub-Saharan work force in 1997, by 2030 this resource-scarce region will have to absorb more than 17 million new entrants each year. Over the next half-century, Nigeria's labour force is projected to grow by 246 per cent and Ethiopia's will soar by 337 per cent—both faster than growth of the general population. At current growth rates, the size of the labour force in sub-Saharan Africa will more than triple by 2050.

As a result of unprecedented population growth and increasing acceptance of female participation in the work force, the number of people seeking jobs in the Middle East and North Africa, a region already plagued by double-digit unemployment rates, will double in the next 50 years. In Algeria, where unemployment stands at 22 per cent, the labour force is growing at a staggering 4.2 per cent annually, and the number seeking work will more than double by 2050. Egypt alone will need to create 26 million more jobs by 2050 as its total population hits 115 million.

Nations throughout Asia will also see phenomenal increases in the numbers seeking work, including Pakistan, where the work force will grow from 70 million in 1998 to 205 million by 2050. Over the next 25 years, India will add nearly 10 million to its work force each year. During the same period, China will add nearly 6 million annually due to population growth alone, compounding the work shortages caused by the current flood of migrants to China's coastal cities and by massive layoffs-estimated at more than 30 million — as state-run operations are scaled back.

Nations are hard-pressed to educate and train rapidly growing numbers of young people in marketable skills for the global workplace. Moreover, meeting the basic needs of a growing population draws scarce foreign exchange and other resources from investments in education and job creation. Throughout the world, young people entering the work force are increasingly faced with unemployment and social marginalization. In most societies, unemployment rates for those under 25 are substantially higher than for older people.

Surplus farmland once served as a traditional source of employment for growing populations, as new land could be plowed to generate work and income. However, global percapita Greenland has dropped by half and considerably more in certain nations since 1950. Moreover, the mechanization of agriculture fuels the exodus of job seekers into the world's urban areas, where unemployment is often most acute. Heavily reliant on natural capital in the past, future job creation will require massive amounts of financial capital to jump-start the industrial and service sectors.

As the balance between the demand and supply of labour is tipped by population growth, wages— the price of labour-tend to decrease. And in a situation of labour surplus, the quality of jobs may not improve as fast for workers will settle for longer hours, fewer benefits and less control over work activities.

Employment is the key to obtaining food, housing, health services, and education, in addition to providing self-respect and self-fulfilment. Rising numbers of unemployed people could drive global poverty and hunger to precarious levels, fueling political instability.

3

Population Growth and Income

Global economic output, the total of all goods, and services produced, grew from $5 trillion in 1950 to $29 trillion in 1998, expanding more than twice as fast as population. This increase of nearly sixfold boosted incomes rather substantially for most of humanity. Growth of the world economy from 1990 to 1997 exceeded the growth during the 10,000 years from the beginning of agriculture until 1950.

Economic output per person climbed from just over @1,900 in 1950 to nearly @5,000 in 1997, a gain of 163 per cent. Although there is an enormous income gap between industrial and developing countries, the latter's economies are growing far more rapidly. Growth in industrial countries has slowed to scarcely 2 per cent a year during the 1990s, compared with nearly 6 per cent a year in developing nations.

The fastest-growing region in the world from 1990 to 1997 was Asia, which averaged nearly 8 per cent annually. This growth was led by China, whose economy has been increasing at nearly 10 per cent a year throughout much of this decade, making it the world's fastest-growing economy. Since 1980, China's economic output has doubled every eight years.

Incomes have risen most rapidly in developing countries where population growth has slowed the most, including, importantly, the countries of East Asia-South Korea, Taiwan, China, Thailand, Indonesia, and Malaysia. Concentrating early on reducing birth rates helped to boost savings to invest in education, health care, and the infrastructure needed by a modern industrial society.

At the other end of the spectrum, African countries—largely ignoring family planning—have been overwhelmed by the sheer numbers of young people who need to be educated and employed. With population growth rates remaining at close to 3 per cent or more a year, most of any economic growth that occurred has been absorbed by the increasing population, leaving little to raise incomes.

The enormous growth during the 1990s, particularly in East Asia, is due to the huge increase in private capital flows into developing countries. Between 1990 and 1997, annual private capital flows increased from $42 billion to $256 billion, a gain of more than sixfold. This substantial amount of money dwarfs traditional flows in public funds under international aid programmes.

Although incomes in much of the developing world are rising rapidly, they are not rising for everyone. The World Bank estimates that 1.3 billion of the world's people subsist on $1 a day or less. For this one-fifth of humanity, trapped at a subhuman level of existence, there has not been any meaningful progress.

The sources of growth are changing. In earlier times, most of the growth was in agriculture. Since the advent of the Industrial Revolution, however, more and more of the growth has been concentrated in industry. Then beginning around mid-century, the services sector-insurance, banking, education-began to expand rapidly, accounting for most of the change in the industrial world. More recently, growth has been concentrated in the information sector as computerization of the economy and telecommunications have grown at extraordinary rates.

The good news is that the global economy has been expanding at a near record pace during the 1990s. The bad news is that the economy, as now structured, is outgrowing the Earth's ecosystem. The result is excessive pressures on the natural systems and resources. As noted in the first section of this paper, from 1950 to 1997 the use of lumber more than doubled. That of paper increased sixfold, the fish catch increased nearly fivefold, grain consumption nearly tripled, fossil fuel burning nearly guandrupled, and air and water pollutants multiplied severalfold. The unfortunate reality is that the economy continues to expand, but the ecosystem on which it depends does not, creating an increasingly stressed relationship.

If the economy were to expand only enough to cover population growth until 2050, it would need to grow from the $29 trillion of 1997 to $47 trillion. This, of course, would merely maintain current incomes, unacceptable though they are for much of humanity. If, on the other hand, the economy were to continue to expand at 3 per cent per year, global economic output would reach $138 trillion in the year 2050.

Even the first, more modest, growth projection would likely lead to a deterioration of the Earth's natural systems to the point where the economy itself would begin to decline. It is easy to foresee a scenario of continuing forest destruction, aquifer depletion, and ecosystem collapse that would lead to economic decline. If the world cannot simultaneously convert the economy to one that is environmentally sustainable—one that does not destroy its own support systems—and move to a lower population trajectory, economic decline will be hard to avoid.

4

Population Growth and Education

In contrast to the food supply challenge posed by the coming wave of population growth, the global need for teachers and classrooms will rise very slowly in the next half-century. In many countries, the school-age population is increasing much less rapidly than the overall national population. The trend illustrates that growth rates typically differ for different age strata of the population. It also shows that declining birth rates can take decades to move through an entire population.

At the global level, for example, total population is projected to increase by 54 per cent between 2000 and 2050, but the number of children aged 5 to 14 will grow by only 6 per cent. And of the world's largest countries—accounting for 60 per cent of global population in 1995—will actually begin to see decreases in the number of children aged 5 to 4 by 2015; for several of these countries, the decline in this age group has already begun. These countries will need fewer classrooms and teachers to educate the youngest members of society (assuming they maintain current class size and student-teacher ratios).

Plenty of nations, however, still have increasing child-age populations. Where countries have not acted to stabilize population, the base of the national population pyramid continues to expand, and pressures on the educational system will be severe. In the world's 10 fastest-growing countries, for example, most of which are in Africa and the Middle East, the child-age population will increase in average 93 per cent over the next half-century. Africa as a whole will see its school-age population grow by 75 per cent through 2040.

The rapid growth in African populations is especially worrisome because of the extra burden it imposes in a region already lagging in education. Only 56 per cent of Africans south of the Sahara are literate, compared with 71 per cent for all developing countries. Few African countries have universal primary education, and secondary education reaches only 4-5 per cent of African children. Educating today's children is challenge enough; the addition of another three students for every four already there will require heroic investments in education. But the alternative is grim: without additional investments in education, today's average student-teacher ratio of 42 in sub-Saharan Africa will reach 75 by 2040.

Many countries will be challenged to increase funding for education while ensuring that other worthy sectors also receive the support they need. With 900 million illiterate adults in the world, the case for a renewed commitment to education is easy to make. But competiting for these funds are the 840 million chronically hungry and the 1.2 billion without access to a decent toilet.

The budget stresses on governments attempting to meet these basic needs would clearly be reduced with smaller populations. Mozambique and lesotho, for example, both met the UNESCO benchmark for investment in education in 1992—6 per cent of gross domestic product—and the two countries economies were roughly equal in size. Yet because Mozambique has many times the population of Lesotho, spending per child in Lesotho is about nine times higher than in Mozambique. For the majority of countries who do not meet the UNESCO funding standard, many of whom also fall short in providing other basic services, a decline in population pressure could help substantially to meet all of their social goals.

If national education systems begin to stress life-long learning for a rapidly changing world, as recommended by a 1998 UNESCO report on education in the twenty-first century, then extensive provision for adult education will be necessary, affecting even those countries with shrinking childage populations. Such a development means that countries that started population stabilization programmes earliest will be in the best position to educate their entire citizenry.

5

Population Growth and Energy

It has been scarcely 200 years — the dawn of the Industrial Revolution—since humans abandoned sole reliance on firewood, other biomass fuels, and direct sunlight to meet daily energy needs. In the past half-century, global demand for energy grew twice as fast as population, as industrial nations burned coal, oil, and natural gas to fuel their economies. Over the next half-century, world energy demands are projected to continue expanding beyond population growth, as developing countries try to catch up with industrial nations.

Developing countries will see tremendous growth in energy consumption in the next half-century, as growing populations and increasing affluence combine to drive their energy demands to dizzying levels. Based on projections from the US Department of Energy and the Intergovernmental Panel of Climate Change, total energy consumption in the developing world will grow by 336 per cent—nearly three times faster than population—over the next 50 years, from 3,499 million tons of oil equivalent to 15,255 million tons. By 2030, energy consumption in the developing world will likely surpass usage in industrial nations.

Rising per capita consumption accounts for nearly two-thirds of the growth in energy demand in poorer nations, but different population trajectories can have dramatic effects on future demands. For example, assuming the same growth in per capita energy demand, moving to the low UN population projection will reduce total energy demands from developing countries by 2,792 million tons of oil equivalent—the output of nearly 3,000 average-sized coal-fired power plants.

In the next 50 years, the greatest growth in energy demands will come where economic activity is projected to be highest: In Asia, where consumption is expected to grow 361 per cent, though population will grow by just 50 per cent. Energy consumption in Latin America and Africa is projected to increase by 340 per cent and 326 per cent, respectively. Lower rates of population growth in Asia, compared with Latin America and Africa, mean that energy use per person will increase most in Asia. Nonetheless, in all three regions, local pressures on energy sources, ranging from forests to fossil fuel reserves to waterways, will be significant.

When per capita energy consumption is high, even a low rate of population growth can have significant effect on total energy demand. In the United States, for example, where current per capita energy demand is nearly double that in other industrial nations and over 13 times that in developing countries, the 75 million people projected to be added in the next 50 years will boost energy demands by 758 million tons of oil equivalent—roughly the same as the present energy consumption of Africa and Latin America.

World energy use per person doubled between 1950 and 1973, before confronting a short-term slowdown when restricted exports from oil-producing nations drove up energy prices. Another price shock, combined with a global economic recession, resulted in the slowdown of the early 1980s. The most recent stumbling block in energy growth followed the 1989 revolution in Eastern Europe, when energy use in the former Soviet states plummeted. Although DOE and IPCC project substantial future growth, similar forces may act to check such a development.

World oil production per person reached a high in 1979 and has since declined 23 per cent. Moreover, estimates of when global oil production will peak range from 2011 by petroconsultants to 2025 by the IPCC, signalling future price shock as long as oil remains the world's dominant fuel. Although people born in 1950 saw per capital oil production quickly double in a few short decades, those born in 2000 are likely to see it cut in half, dropping below 1950 levels.

In addition, meeting increased energy demands will require more storage and transportation infrastructure. Communities without a reliable supply of clean water or an adequate system for waste disposal may also fall short in connection to power supplies. For the estimated 2 billion who are still off the grid—and also experiencing high rates of population growth—decentralized energy technologies, such as solar roof shingles and fuel cell power generators, are likely the most feasible and affordable option for meeting increased energy demands.

Yet it will not necessarily be the scarcity of fuel that constrains future growth in energy consumption, but rather concerns about climate change, air quality, and water quality. Growing climate concerns will require massive reductions in fossil fuel use at a time when demand for energy is soaring. A shift to renewable energy sources, such as solar energy and wind power, in addition to continued efficiency gains for power plants, cars, and appliances, holds great promise for meeting future energy demands without adverse ecological consequences.

6

Population Growth and Cropland

Since mid-century, global population has grown much faster than the cropland area. The trend is likely to continue in the next century, dropping cropland per person to historically low levels. The ever smaller per capita cropland base will make food self-sufficiency impossible for many countries, and will test the capacity of international markets to meet a growing demand for imported food.

For millennia, farmers satisfied rising food demand by bringing new land under the plow. But by mid-century cropland expansion could no longer meet the food needs of an increasingly populous and prosperous world. The 10,000 year era of steady expansion was over, and a new era began that stressed raising land productivity. As this high-yielding era shows signs of faltering, concern over the shrinking supply of cropland per person looms ever larger.

Since mid-century, grain area—which serves as a proxy for cropland in general—has increased by some 19 per cent, but global population has grown 132 per cent, seven times faster. Largely as a result, grain area per person has fallen by half since 1950, from 0.24 to 0.12 hectares. Assuming that grain area remains constant, grain area per person will fall to 0.07 hectares by 2050. In crowded industrial countries such as Japan, Taiwan, and South Korea, grain area per capita today is smaller than the area of a tennis court.

As grain area per person falls, more and more nations risk losing the capacity to feed themselves. Having already seen per capita grain area shrink by 40-50 per cent between 1960 and 1998, Pakistan, Nigeria, Ethiopia, and Iran can expect a further 60-70 per cent loss by 2050—a conservative projection that assumes no further losses of agricultural land. The result will be four countries with a combined population of more than 1 billion whose grain area per person will be only 300-600 square metres, less than a quarter of the area in 1950.

The historical record suggests that such a small area per person will send a substantial share of a country's people to world markets from their food. Consider the experience of six countries in East Asia whose per capita grain area currently ranges from 200 to 600 square metres per person. Sri Lanka relies on imports for more than a third of its grain, while Japan, Taiwan, South Korea, and Malaysia buy more than 70 per cent of their grain form abroad. North Korea is the only one of the six that does not import heavily (it gets less than 20 per cent of its grain requirements from abroad), but its population is poorly fed-indeed, on the verge of starvation.

The concern is that population growth will push many nations—not just the four fastest-growing ones—below the 600 square metre-threshold in coming decades. In Asia alone, where grain area per person stands at 800 square metres, 16 countries are poised to cross this threshold by 2050, and many of them much sooner. As this process unfolds, the number of people who will turn to foreign markets for their food will likely jump sharply. These countries will find an increasingly tight international grain market, with nations from the Middle East, North Africa, and other regions already buying a third or more of their grain overseas.

In addition to per capita losses, population growth can lead to degradation of cropland, reducing its productivity or even eliminating it from production. As a country's population density increases and good farmland becomes scarce, poor farmers are forced onto ecologically vulnerable land such as hillsides and tropical forest. In the Philippines, for example, hillside agriculture accounted for only 10 per cent of all agricultural land in 1960, but 30 per cent in 1987. Because it is highly erodible, hillside land is easily damaged; worldwide, some 160 million hectares of hillside farmland—11 per cent of cropland—were characterized in 1989 as 'severely eroded.' Similarly, population pressure can force peasants to overfarm the poor soils of tropical forests. After being cleared and farmed for a few years, these soils typically require fallow periods of 20-25 years, but population pressures keep poor farmers on the same land for far longer than the soil can support, cutting fallow periods to just a few years in some areas of tropical Africa and Asia.

Finally, population pressures on a fixed base of land can result in rural landlessness. In Bangladesh, for example, landlessness among rural households rose from 35 per cent in 1960 to 53 per cent in the early 1990s. Interestingly, Bangladesh is regarded as a success in slowing population expansion, as its growth rate declined from 2.8 per cent in the late 1970s to 1.5 per cent in the early 1990s. But its success came too late to prevent the increase in rural landlessness, highlighting the need to work sooner, rather than later, for population stabilization.

7

Population Growth and Meat Production

World meat production increased from 44 million tons almost twice as fast as population. In per capita terms, world meat production expanded from 17 kilograms in 1950 to 36 kilograms in 1997, more than doubling. Growth in meat production was originally concentrated in western industrial countries and Japan, but over the last two decades it has increased rapidly in East Asia (especially China), the Middle East, and Latin America.

When incomes begin to rise in traditional low-income societies, one of the first things people do is diversify their diets, consuming more livestock products. People everywhere appear to have an innate desire to consume at least moderate quantities of meat, perhaps reflecting our evolutionary history as hunter-gatherers.

Three types of meat—beef, pork, and poultry—account for the bulk of world consumption; mutton ranks a distant fourth. From 1950 until 1980, beef and pork production followed the same trend, but after the economic reforms in China—where pork is dominant—pork production surged ahead, climbing from 45 million tons to nearly 90 million tons in less than two decades.

Historically, growth in the world meat supply came primarily from beef and mutton, sustained by the world's rangelands. These areas, consisting mostly of land that is too arid to support crop production, cover a vast part of the planet, roughly double the cropland area. Not only do the herds of cattle and flocks of sheep and goats provide meat and milk, but for millions of people in Africa, the Middle East, Central Asia, parts of the Indian subcontinent, and western China, they provide a livelihood. The only feasible way that this land can contribute to the world's food supply is to graze cattle, sheep, and goats on it, producing the meat and milk that directly and indirectly sustain large segment of humanity.

In recent years, beef and mutton production have levelled off at just over 60 million tons per year as the number of animals has pressed against the carrying capacity of range lands. With little unused grazing capacity left, future gains in meat production will have to come largely from feeding animals grain. At this point, the relative conversion efficiency of various animals begins to influence production trends. Producing a kilogram of beef in the feedlot requires roughly seven kilograms of grain, while a kilogram of pork requires nearly four of grain and a kilogram of poultry, just over two. As grain supplies tighten, the advantage shifts from beef to pork and even more so to poultry. This helps explain why world poultry production overtook that of beef in 1996.

Of the world grain harvest of 1.87 billion tons in 1998, an estimated 37 per cent—or nearly 700 million tons—will be used to feed livestock and poultry, producing milk and eggs as well as meat. This share, remarkably stable for the last decade, could go up or down depending on future grain prices.

Expanding world meat production also depends on soybean production. If the grain fed to livestock or poultry is supplemented with a modest amount of soybean meal (the high protein meal that is left after the oil is extracted), its conversion into meat is much more efficient. Largely as a result of this growing demand for livestock products, world soybean production climbed from 17 million tons in 1950 to 152 million tons in 1997, a gain of ninefold.

To project the future demand for meat, we assume that the growth in meat consumption per person will slow over the next half-century, rising by one half instead of doubling, since some countries are nearing the saturation point. This, combined with the projected growth in population, would push total meat consumption from 211 million tons in 1997 to 513 million tons in 2050, a gain of 302 million tons. If we assume an average of 3 kilograms of grain per kilogram of meat produced, this would require more than 900 million tons of additional grain for feed in 2050, an amount equal to half of current world grain consumption. This would greatly intensify the competition between grain consumed directly and that consumed indirectly as animal protein, calling into question whether such gains in meat consumptions will ever materialize.

Grain fed to livestock and poultry is now the principal food reserve in the event of a world food emergency. As of 1990, the world had, in effect, three reserves in the global food system: substantial stocks of grain that could be drawn upon in the event of unexpected shortages, a large area of cropland idled under US farm commodity programmes, and grain fed to animals. By 1998, world grain stocks had been depleted to one of the lowest levels on record and the cropland that was idled for half a century was returned to production. The only safety net remaining in the event of a major crop failure is the grain fed to livestock and poultry.

8

Population Growth and Urbanization

The world's cities are growing far faster than its population. Indeed, aside from the growth of population itself, urbanization is the dominant demographic trend of the half-century now ending. In 1950, 750 million of the world's people lived in cities. By 1996, this had at least tripled, to more than 2.6 billion. The number projected to live in cities by 2050, some 6.5 billion people, exceeds world population today.

Urbanization on anything like the scale that we know today is historically quite recent. In 1800, only one city—London—had a million people. Today, 326 cities have at least that many people. And there are 14 megacities, those with 10 million or more residents. Tokyo is the largest, at 27 million. Mexico City is second, at 17 million. New York City and Sao Paulo are close behind, with 16 million each. Rounding out the list in descending size are Mumbai

(15 million), Shanghai (14), Los Angeles (12), Calcutta (12), Buenos Aires (12), Beijing (11), Osaka (11), Lagos (10), Rio de Janeiro (10), and Delhi (10).

The rate of growth of cities in industrial countries during the first century or so of the Industrial Revolution was relatively slow. Today's cities are growing much faster. It took London 130 years to get from 1 million to 8 million. Mexico City made this jump in just 30 years.

Measured in annual growth, some cities, such as Lagos, Nigeria, are growing at 5 per cent a year; Mumbai is growing at nearly 4 per cent. The world's urban population as a whole is growing by just over 1 million people each weak. This urban growth is fed by the natural increase of urban populations, by net migration from the countryside, and by villages, by not migration from the countryside, and by villages or towns expanding to the point where they become cities or they are absorbed by the spread of existing cities.

During the early stages of industrialization, urbanization was largely in response to the pull of employment opportunities in cities. More recently, however, the movement from countryside to city has been more the result of rural push than of urban pull. It is a reflection of the lack of opportunity in the countryside as already small plots of land are divided and then divided again with each passing generation, until they become so small that people can no longer make a living from them.

Historically, cities and the surrounding countryside had a symbolic relationship, with the latter supplying food and raw materials in exchange for manufactured products. Today cities are tied much more to each other and to the global economy. The food and fuel that once came from the surrounding countryside now often comes from distant corners of the planet.

As societies urbanize, the use of basic resources, such as energy, and water, rises. In traditional rural societies, for example, people live on the land and thus do not need to travel to work. But once they migrate to cities, commuting becomes the rule, not the exception. In villages, most of the food that is consumed is produced locally, requiring little energy for processing, packaging, and transportation; once people move into cities, on the other hand, virtually all their food must be brought in. In a village where residents typically draw their water from a central well and carry it to their homes, water use is necessarily limited. But when villagers move to urban high-rise apartment buildings with indoor plumbing, replete with showers and flush toilets, water consumption soars.

The ecology of cities is a continuing challenge to city managers simply because cities require the concentration of huge quantities of water, food, energy and raw materials. The waste products must then be dispersed or the city will become uninhabitable. As cities become larger, the disposal of residential and industrial wastes becomes ever more challenging.

Partly as a result of the mounting pressure for people to migrate to cities, the growth in urban populations is far outstripping the availability of basic services, such as water, sewerage, transportation, and electricity. As a result, life in urban shantytowns is plagued by poverty, pollution, congestion, homelessness, and unemployment.

Since the beginning of the Industrial Revolution, the terms of trade between countryside and city have favoured the latter simply because cities control the scarce resources in development, namely capital and technology. But if the price of food rises in the years ahead, as now seems likely, the terms of trade could shift, favouring the countryside. If in the new world of the twenty-first century the scarce resources are land and water, those controlling them could have the upper hand in determining rural/urban terms of trade.

This aside, if recent trends continue, within the next several years more than half of us will be living in cities—making the world more urban than rural for the first time in history. We will have become an urban species, far removed from our hunter-gatherer origins.

9

Population Growth and Natural Recreation Areas

Population growth during the past 50 years has made it difficult to set aside and conserve natural areas. Another half-century of growth will put even more pressure on protected areas as formerly small, distant settlements encroach on these sites and as the number of people (both local and visitors) who use these sites explodes.

National parks, forests, wildlife preserves, beaches, and other protected areas offer sanctuary to various habitats and indigenous communities, in addition to providing resources for local peoples. In an urbanizing world, these sites provide an opportunity for healthy interaction with the natural environment, as well as rare serenity.

From Buenos Aires to Bangkok, dramatic population growth in the world's major cities and the sprawl and population they bring—threatens natural recreation areas that lay beyond city limits.

Tremendous growth in the population of Mumbai has already engulfed Borivili National Park, a reserve that was beyond the city's periphery only a decade ago. With projected growth of 60 per cent in the next 20 years, Mumbai may soon swallow up more distant areas. On every continent, human encroachment has reduced both the size and the quality of natural recreation areas.

In nations where rapid population growth has outstripped the carrying capacity of local resources, protected areas become especially vulnerable. Although in industrial nations these areas are synonymous with camping, hiking, and picnics in the country, in Asia, Africa and Latin America most national parks, forests, and preserves are inhabited or used for natural resources by local populations.

An assessment by the World Conservation Union-IUCN of 30 protected sites in the developing world shows that these areas now act as magnets, attracting people to the rich oasis of water, fuel, food, and other resources they contain. Population growth rates in and around these areas are typically 2 percentage points above the national average-largely as a result of immigration from resource-starved areas.

As people seek out scarce resources, the resulting concentrations can be devastating. For example, population densities in the region surrounding Bwindi Impenetrable National Park in southern Uganda are some of the highest in all of Africa—exceeding 250 people for square kilometres. Though population at this site is expected to multiply, chronic land hunger already precipitates conflicts over fuel-wood collection, farming, cattle grazing, and bush burning.

Migration-driven population growth also endangers natural recreation areas in many industrial nations. Everglades National

Park faces collapse as millions of newcomers move into South Florida.

Coastal recreation areas, including beaches, may be most burdened by the formidable combination of population growth and migration. All but one of the world's 15 largest cities—Mexico City—are coastal, and all of these cities will grow in the decades ahead. Whether it takes the form of expanding shantytowns in Kingston, Jamaica, or sprawling tract housing in southern California, virtually all the growth and movement in population in the next 50 years will occur in densely populated coastal corridors.

In nations already struggling to meet basic human needs, the prospect of establishing additional protected areas becomes increasingly slim. Throughout India, for example, while the national government designates areas as protected, state and local governments work to de-reserve these sites so that the resources can be harnessed to meet the needs of an additional 18 million Indians each year.

Sunbathers on beaches in Japan are often compared to sardines. People who use Central Park in New York City, which has nearly doubled in population since 1950, are faced with growing congestion and restrictions on activities. National parks throughout North America are confronted with huge backlogs of requests to visit, having to turn tourists away. Tourism at Yosemite has boomed from roughly 4,000 visitors in 1886 to more than 4 million people (and their cars) today. It is often remarked that 'Americans love their national parks to death', as increased visitation degrades campsites, trails, and wilderness.

Longer waiting lists and higher user fees for fewer secluded spots are likely the tip of the iceberg, as population growth threatens to eliminate the diversity of habitats and cultures, in addition to the peace and quiet, that protected areas currently house.

10

Population Growth and Housing

Over the past half-century, the world's housing stock has grown roughly in step with population. Yet for more and more people worldwide, adequate and affordable housing remains beyond reach, driving some into substandard dwellings and slums and others onto the street. This situation stands to worsen, for the need for housing worldwide is projected to nearly double over the next 50 years.

Although industrial nations currently occupy a disproportionately large share of the world's households relative to their population, virtually all future growth will occur in developing countries, where housing requirements will more than double by the middle of the twenty-first century. This phenomenal growth results from the potent synergy between population growth and a shift toward fewer people per household—a trend that is especially pronounced where economic growth is rapid.

HABITAT, the United Nations Centre for Human Settlements, has projected housing requirements based on roughly a 30-per cent reduction in people per household over the next 50 years. These figures are purely statistical estimates and do not consider possible checks in housing growth, such as materials or financial constraints, intensified land competition, or increased poverty. Our own projections assume that household size will indeed decrease, as fertility rates drop and as extended families become more rare, but by a more modest 15 per cent.

Over the next 50 years, housing needs in Africa and the Middle East are expected to increase more than threefold, with tremendous gains in the region's most populous nations; demands are to increase 3.5 times in Nigeria and 4.5 times in Ethiopia. Although less dramatic percentage increases are expected in Asia, the doubling of households in the region will require nearly 700 million additional homes by 2050. Still, some countries there, such as Pakistan and neighbouring Afghanistan, will see housing needs increase nearly three and a half times.

The projected growth in housing needs becomes all the more daunting given that rapid population growth—combined with rapid urban growth—has already left a large share of the world's population without adequate housing. HABITAT estimates that at least 600 million urban dwellers and more than 1 billion rural dwellers in Africa, Asia, and Latin America live in housing that is so overcrowded and of such poor quality with such inadequate provision for water, sanitation, drainage, and garbage collection that their lives and their health are continually at risk.

As the supply of housing falls behind demand, the quality of available housing tends to deteriorate. Cheaper, less durable materials, such as scrap metal and cardboard, are substituted for more expensive, weather-resistant materials, such as concrete and wood. Fierce competition in swelling urban areas for desirable land can eliminate all hope of low-income households acquiring a plot for housing. As choice of location dwindles, shantytowns and other low-quality settlements develop on marginal land ill suited for housing-in floodplains, on steep hillsides, near garbage dumps or other environmentally risky sites. From New York to Beijing, cities are faced with land and materials constraints even as their populations continue to grow.

At the same time, housing area per person continues to increase in certain nations and among the more affluent segments of other nations, placing additional stress on prime space and building materials. In the United States, Western Europe, and Japan—a nation traditionally known for small dwellings-floor space per person has more than doubled in new single family homes since mid-century. The global disparity in floor space per person—Washington, D.C., at the high end with 70 square metres per person, and most of humanity at around 9 square metres per person—will likely mimic the growing global disparity in income, as wealthy households scale up and poorer households fill up.

Housing can provide a connection to a supply of fresh water and sanitation facilities. But as its quality deteriorates, so do these basic amenities. Half the world's people are without access to sanitation and nearly this many—2.7 billion—are without a reliable source of safe drinking water. Shortages of housing that provides these basic services are most acute in cities, where rapid urbanization and high population densities place heightened demands on infrastructure.

And still housing needs are projected to soar in the regions of the world where access to water and sanitation are most constrained.

The ultimate manifestation of population growth outstripping the supply of housing is homelessness. The United Nations estimates that at least 100 million of the world's people—roughly the same as the population of Mexico have no home; the number tops 1 billion if those with especially insecure or temporary accommodations, such as squatters, are included. In many developing countries, squatter communities are home to 30-60 per cent of the urban population. There are some 250,000 pavement dwellers in Mumbai alone. Humans who are born, live, and die in the streets—are common in all major cities. Unless the world moves to a lower population trajectory, the ranks of homeless are likely to swell dramatically.

11

Population Growth and Forests

Global losses of forest area have marched in step with population growth for much of human history. The two trends rose slowly for millennia, turned upward in recent centuries, and accelerated sharply after 1900. Indeed, 75 per cent of the historical growth in global population and an estimated 75 per cent of the loss in global forested area have occurred in the twentieth century. The correlation makes sense, given the additional need for farmland, pastureland, and forest products as human numbers expand. But since 1950, the advent of mass consumption of forest products has quickened the pace of deforestation.

In some cases, population pressure is still closely linked with deforestation. In Latin America, for example, ranching is the single largest cause of deforestation. Because most meat produced in Latin America is consumed there, and because meat consumption per person has been largely unchanged for several decades, it is likely that expanding population is the principal reason for ranching-related deforestation. In addition, analysts at the World Resources Institute estimate that overgrazing and overcollection of firewood—which are often a function of a growing population—are degrading some 14 per cent of the world's threatened frontier forests (large areas of virgin forest). In fact, a UN Food and Agriculture Organization study showed a one-to-one correlation between population growth and fuelwood consumption in 16 Asian countries between 1961 and 1994.

On the other hand, deforestation created by the demand for forest products tracks more closely with rising per capita consumption in recent decades. Global use of paper and paperboard per person, for example, has doubled (or nearly tripled) since 1961, and most of the increase has come in wealthy countries with low or even stable levels of population growth. Europe, Japan, and North America, with 16 per cent of global population, consume 63 per cent of the world's paper and paperboard and nearly half its industrial wood.

Although consumption and population growth have operated somewhat independently in the late twentieth century, the two forces could coincide in the developing world in coming decades, with substantial consequences for forests. Developing country paper consumption is less than one-tenth the level found in industrial nations, suggesting that large increases in consumption are likely as these nations prosper. (It also suggests that greater economy is needed in industrial countries). With 80 per cent of the world's people, and as home to all the increase in population in coming decades, even modest growth in per capital paper and wood consumption in developing countries could place substantial pressure on forests. If paper were used by the entire world in 2050 at today's industrial-nation rates, paper production would need to jump more than eightfold over 1996 levels.

This projected growth is unsustainable, given that global use of forest products is already near or beyond the limits of sustainable use. Using data on sustainable forest yields, and assuming that virgin forests are left intact, researchers at Friends of the Earth UK have determined that production of forest products for the world is 25 per cent beyond the most restrictive estimates for sustainable consumption. (Many forests, of course, are already logged well beyond sustainable levels). The most optimistic assessment would allow for a further 35-per cent growth in consumption. Even that spells trouble, however, given a projected global population increase of some 54 per cent over the next half-century, and given the likely increase in consumption from rising prosperity. Lower consumption of forest products and increased recycling in industrial countries can make room for a more prosperous developing world to enjoy the products of the world's forests, but the task will be made easier if population growth everywhere is stabilized sooner rather than later.

If population and consumption eat into the world's forests, the resulting loss of forest services reduces, in turn, a country's capacity to support its population. Forests provide habitat to a diverse selection of wildlife; tropical forests, for example, are home to more than 50 per cent of the world's species. And as store houses of carbon, forests are key to regulating climate. Deforestation leads to huge releases of carbon: an estimated one quarter of the world's carbon emissions come from forest clearing. Loss of these macroservices undermines the stability and resiliency of the global environment on which economies—and populations—depend. In addition, forests provide services vital to a local population, such as control of erosion, steady provision of water across rainy and dry seasons, and regulation of rainfall. Taken together, the loss of these services due to deforestation can upset local economies and subject local populations to economic instability.

12

Population Growth and Biodiversity

As human population has surged this century, the populations of numerous other species have tumbled, many to the point of extinction. Indeed, we live amid the greatest extinction of plant and animal life since the dinosaurs disappeared some 65 million years ago, with species losses at 100 to 1,000 times the natural rate. But humans are not just witnesses to a rare historic event, we are actually its cause. The leading sources of today's species loss, habitat alteration, invasions by exotic species, pollution, and overhunting are all a function of human activities.

Human activities have pushed the percentage of mammals, amphibians, land fish that are in 'immediate danger' of extinction into double digits. The principal cause of species extinction is habitat loss—the result of encroachment by humans for settlements, for agriculture, or to claim resources such as timber. A particularly productive but vulnerable habitat is found in coastal areas, home to 60 per cent of the world's population. Coastal wetlands nurture two-thirds of all commercially caught fish, for example. And coral reefs have the second highest concentration of biodiversity in the world, after tropical rainforests. But human encroachment and pollution are degrading these areas: roughly half of the world's salt marshes and mangrove swamps have been eliminated or radically altered, and two-thirds of the world's coral reefs have been degraded, 10 per cent of them 'beyond recognition'. As coastal migration continues—coastal dweiiers could account for 75 per cent of world population within 30 years—the pressures on these productive habitats will likely increase.

Habitat loss tends to accelerate with an increase in a country's population density. This is bad news for the world's biodiversity hotspots-species-rich ecosystems at greatest risk of destruction. Twenty-four of these hotspots, containing half of the planet's species, have been identified globally. Some of the most important hotspot countries will reach population densities that have been linked with very high rates of habitat loss. Five of the six most biologically rich countries could see more than two-thirds of their original habitat destroyed by 2050 if this historical relationship holds.

Related to loss of habitat is the growing incidence of plant, animal, insect, and microbial invasions of ecosystems worldwide as human interchange increases. These 'exotic species' sometimes dominate local ecosystems, eliminating native species and reducing overall diversity. Exotics are implicated in 68 per cent of all fish extinctions in the United States this century, for example. Growth in human travel and commerce explains many accidental invasions by exotics, but foreign species are also deliberately introduced into farms, plantation forests, and aquaculture systems. Although only 1 per cent of exotics cause widespread damage, exotic species are the second leading cause, after habitat destruction, of species loss worldwide.

Other, often difusre effects of expanded human activities also disrupt ecosystems. Nitrogen, for example, is now made available to plants at more than twice the pre-industrial rate as a result of fertilizer production, cultivation of nitrogen-fixing crops, and the burning of fossil fuels. This overfertilization of the Earth favours some species at the expense of others, leading to a reduction in diversity and resiliency of land and aquatic ecosystems.

Likewise, greenhouse gas emissions could distrupt ecosystems on a vast scale. As with nitrogen, increased levels of atmospheric carbon may favour some species over others: annuals over perennials, for example, or deciduous trees over evergreens. To the extent that greenhouse gases induce changes in global climate, many species may be at risk as habitats shift or shrink, and as some life forms, such as insects or animals, adapt and migrate more quickly than others, such as plants. And as sea levels rise with a change in climate, ecosystems such as coastal wetlands could be destroyed.

13

Population Growth and Grain Production

The relationship between the growth in world population and the grain harvest has shifted over the last half-century, neatly dividing this period into two distinct eras. From 1950 to 1984, growth and the grain harvest easily exceeded that of population, raising the harvest per person from 247 kilograms to 342, a gain of 38 per cent. During the 14 years since then, growth in the grain harvest has fallen behind that of population, dropping output per person from its historic high in 1984 to an estimated 317 kilograms in 1998—a decline of 7 per cent, or 0.5 per cent a year.

These global trends conceal widely divergent developments among countries, contrasts that can be seen for the world's two most populous nations: India and China. In both, grain production per person was close to 200 kilograms as recently as 1978. Since then, the figure in India has edged up slightly but still falls short of

200 kilograms, while in China production has surged since the economic reforms in 1978, with per-person output now at nearly 300 kilograms. The combination of a dramatic surge in grain production and an equally dramatic reduction in population growth has given China a large margin of safety, effectively eliminating most of its hunger and malnutrition. Meanwhile, although India has also achieved impressive gains in its harvest, these have been largely cancelled by population growth, leaving its 976 million people living close to the margin.

What has happened in China and India is the story of developing countries in general. The overwhelming majority have achieved substantial, if not dramatic, gains in their grain harvests over the last half-century. Some, such as Thailand, have combined this with a much slower growth of population, which means that agricultural gains translate into rising grain production per person. In Pakistan, by contrast, grain production per person climbed steadily for awhile, but it peaked in 1981 at 186 kilograms. Since then it has been declining nearly 1 per cent a year. In effect, Pakistan's farmers are losing the battle with population growth.

The slower growth in the world grain harvest since 1984 is due to the lack of new land and to slower growth in irrigation and fertilizer use. Irrigated area per person, after expanding by 4 per cent since then as growth in the irrigated area has fallen behind that of population.

The increase in world fertilizer use has slowed dramatically since 1990, as diminishing returns to the application of additional fertilizer has stabilized use in the United States, Western Europe, and Japan and slowed annual growth in world fertilizer use from 6 per cent between 1950 and 1990 to scarcely 2 per cent in recent years.

Although Malthus was primarily concerned with the additional demand for grain generated by population growth, rising affluence is also playing a role. In a low income country such as India, grain consumption per person is less than 200 kilograms per year and diets are typically dominated by a single starchy staple-rice, for instance. With scarcely a pound of grain available a day per person, nearly all must be consumed directly, leaving little for conversion into animal protein. For the average American, on the other hand, the great bulk of the 800-kilogram daily grain consumption is taken in indirectly in the form of beef, pork, poultry, eggs, milk, cheese, ice cream, and yogurt. At the intermediate level, in a country like Italy, people consume 400 kilograms of grain a day. Future food price stability thus depends on expanding production fast enough to keep up with both population growth and rising affluence.

One question often asked is, How many people can the Earth support? This must be answered with another question, At what level of consumption? If the world grain harvest of 1.87 billion tons were expanded to 2 billion tons in the years ahead, it would support 10 billion Indians or 2.5 billion Americans. To answer the question of how many people the Earth can support, we first have to know the level of consumption we expect to live at.

Now that the frontiers of agricultural settlement have disappeared, future growth in grain production must come almost entirely from raising land productivity. Unfortunately, this is becoming more difficult. After rising at 2.1 per cent a year from 1950 to 1990, the annual increase in rainland productivity dropped to scarcely 1 per cent from 1990 to 1997. The challenge for the world's farmers is to reverse this decline at a time when cropland area per person is shrinking, the amount of irrigation water per person is dropping, and the crop yield response to additional fertilizer use is falling.

14

Population Growth and Fresh Water

Wherever population is growing, the supply of fresh water per person is declining. As a result of population growth, the amount of water available per person from the hydrological cycle will fall by 74 per cent between 1950 and 2050. Stated otherwise, there will be only one-fourth as much fresh water per person in 2050 as there was in 1950. With water availability per person projected to decline dramatically in many countries already facing shortages, the full social effects of future water scarcity are difficult even to imagine. Indeed, spreading water scarcity may be the most underrated resource issue in the world today.

Evidence of water stress can be seen as rivers are drained dry and as water tables fall. The Colorado River in the southwestern United States now rarely reaches the sea. The Yellow River, the northernmost of China's two major rivers, has run dry for a part of each year since 1985, with the dry period becoming progressively longer. In 1997, it failed to make it to the sea for 226 days. The Nile, the largest river in the Middle East, has little water left when it reaches the sea.

Water tables are now falling on every continent including in major food-producing regions. Among those where aquifers are being depleted are the US Southern Great Plains the North China Plain, which produces nearly 40 per cent of China's grain; and most of India. Wherever water tables are falling today, there will be water supply cutbacks tomorrow, as aquifers are eventually depleted.

Some 70 per cent of the water pumped from underground or diverted from rivers is used for irrigation, 20 per cent is used for industrial purposes, and 10 per cent is for residential use. Water use patterns vary widely by region. In Europe, for example, where agriculture is largely rainfed, water withdrawals are dominated by industrial use. In Asia, in contrast, irrigation accounts for 85 per cent of all water use.

As countries press against the limits of their water supplies, the competition among sectors itensifies. The economics of water use does not favor agriculture. One thousand tons of water can be used to produce one ton of wheat worth $200 or to expand industrial output by $14,000. This ratio of 70 to 1 explains why industry almost always wins in the competition with agriculture for water.

As the growing demand for water collides with the limits of supply, countries typically satisfy rising urban and residential demands by diverting water from irrigation. They then import grain to offset the loss of irrigation water. Since it takes at least 1,000 tons of water to produce a ton of grain, importing grain becomes the most efficient way to import water. North Africa and the Middle East—a region where population growth is rapid and every country faces water shortages—has become the world's fastest growing grain import market during the 1990s. In 1997, the water required to produce the grain and other foodstuffs imported into the region was roughly equal to the annual flow of the Nile River.

In both China and India, the two countries that together dominate world irrigated agriculture, substantial cutbacks in irrigation water supplies lie ahead. The combination of the effects of aquifer depletion in key countries such as these and the growing diversion of irrigation water to nonfarm uses in many countries makes it unlikely that there will be much, if any, increase in total irrigated area over the long term. Already the irrigated area per person has been slowly declining since 1978, falling from a historical high of 0.047 hectares per person to 0.045 hectares in 1996—a drop of 4 per cent. If the total irrigated area remains at roughly 263 million hectares until 2050, this key figure will fall to 0.028 hectares per person in 2050—declining by an additional 38 per cent. Such a shrinkage will pose a formidable challenge to the world's farmers.

About a billion people will be living in countries facing absolute water scarcity by 2025. These nations do not have enough water to maintain 1990 levels of food production per person from irrigated area, even with high irrigation efficiency, and to meet the needs for domestic, industrial and environmental purposes as well. They will have to reduce water use in agriculture in order to satisfy residential and industrial water needs. The resulting decline in domestic food production will force them to import more food, assuming it is available. Although detailed water projections by sector for each country are not available for 2050, the number of water-deprived people will be far greater than in 2025 if the world continues on the UN medium population trajectory. The bottom line is that if we are facing a future of water scarcity, then we are also facing future of food scarcity.

15

Population Growth and Oceanic Fish Catch

From 1950 until 1988, the oceanic fish catch soared from 19 million to 88 million tons, expanding much faster than population. The per capita catch increased from less than 8 kilograms in 1950 to the historical peak of just over 17 kilograms in 1988, more than doubling. Since 1988, however, growth in the catch has slowed, falling behind that of population. Between 1988 and 1996, the catch per person declined to less than 16 kilograms, a drop of some 9 per cent.

This fivefold growth in the human appetite for seafood since 1950 has pushed the catch of most oceanic fisheries to their sustainable limits or beyond. Marine biologists believe that the oceans cannot sustain an annual catch of much more than 93 million tons, the current take.

As we near the end of the twentieth century, overfishing has become the rule, not the exception. Of the 15 major oceanic fisheries. 11 are in decline. The catch of Atlantic cod-long a dietary mainstay for West Europeans—has fallen by some 70 per cent since peaking in 1968. Since 1970, bluefin tuna stocks in the West Atlantic have dropped 80 per cent.

The next half-century is likely to be marked by the disappearance of some species from markets, a decline in the quality of seafood caught, higher prices, and more conflicts among countries over access to fisheries. Over the last two decades, a growing share of the catch has consisted of inferior species, some of which were not even considered edible in times past.

The growing scarcity of the species at the top of the food chain is reflected in raising prices. Poor people who once ate fish because they could not afford meat now find that meat is often less expensive than seafood. Although most price rises are moderate, some are extreme–going far beyond anything we could have earlier imagined. The decline of the bluefin tuna population in the Atlantic, for instance, has occasionally pushed prices for a 300-Kilogram tuna above $80,000 at top-of-the-line sushi restaurants in Japan compete for the few of these giant fish that are available.

This growing competition for limited resources has led to ongoing conflicts among countries. The United Nations recorded more than 100 such disputes in 1997. There are evident in the cod wars between Norwegian and Icelandic ships, between Canada and Spain over turbot off Canada's eastern coast, between China and the Marshall Islands in Micronesia, between Argentina and Taiwan over Falkland island fisheries, and between Indonesia and the Philippines in the Celebes. There are "tuna wars in the northeast Atlantic, crab wars in the North Pacific, squid wars in the southwest Atlantic, salmon wars in the North Pacific, and pollock wars in the Sea of Okhotsk." Although these disputes make it into the world news only rarely, they are now an almost daily occurrence. Indeed, historians may record more fishery conflicts during one year in the 1990s than during the entire nineteenth century.

One of the consequences of modern fishing technologies, whether it is the use of drift nets or bottom scouring fish—catch of unwanted species. This oceanic equivalent of clearcutting is damaging fisheries on an unprecedented scale.

With the oceans now pushed to their limits, future growth in the demand for seafood can be satisfied only by fish farming. As a result, aquacultural output has increased from 7 million tons in 1984 to an estimated 26 million tons in 1977. Most of this growth in catch is based on just a few species, such as carp, which constitute most of the aquacultural harvest in China, and catfish, which dominates fish farming in the United States. As the world turns to fish farming to satisfy its needs, fish begin to compete with livestock and poultry for foodstuffs such as grain, soybean meal, and fish meal.

Given that the oceanic fish catch is apparently now at or beyond its sustainable limit, it is a relatively simple matter to determine the future oceanic catch per person. With each year, this will decline by roughly the amount of population growth, dropping to 9.9 kilograms per person in 2050, a decline to little more than half the 1988 peak of 17.2 kilograms. Those of us born before 1950 have enjoyed a doubling of the seafood catch per person, while those born in recent years are likely to witness a decline of nearly one half during their lifetimes.

16

Population Growth and Waste

A growing population increases society's disposal headaches—the garbage, sewage, and industrial waste that must be gotten rid of. Even where population is largely stable—the case in many industrial countries—the flow of waste products into landfills and waterways generally continues to increase in coming decades, as they will in many developing countries, mountains of waste will likely pose difficult disposal challenges for municipal and national authorities.

Data for waste generation in the developing world are scarce, but citizens in many of these countries are estimated to produce roughly half a kilo of municipal waste each day. If this figure is applied to today's population, a total of 824 million tons of municipal waste is being churned out annually in developing countries. Population growth alone would boost this number to 1.5 billion tons by 2050. But waste rates tend to climb with rising incomes; a developing world generating as much waste per capital as industrial countries do today would be producing some 3.6 billion tons of municipal waste in 2050. Moreover, prosperity boosts the volume of waste as the share of plastics, metal, paper, and other nonorganics rises.

Local and global environmental effects of waste disposal will likely worsen as 3.4 billion people are added to global population over the next half-century. Acids from organic wastes, for example, and poisons from hazardous wastes often leach from landfills, polluting local groundwater supplies. And rotting organic matter generates methane, a greenhouse gas. If the waste is incinerated rather than thrown into landfills, cities will have to worry about increases in cancer-causing dioxin emissions, one of the byproducts of burning garbage.

Meanwhile, today's largely unmet sanitation needs could also be greatly exacerbated by population growth. Half the world's people do not have access to a decent toilet, according to UNESCO and the World Health Organization. Lack of sanitation a leading cause of disease: Who reports that half the developing world suffers from one of the six diseases associated with poor water supply and sanitation. One of these, diarrhea, is the biggest killer of children today, taking an estimated 2.2 million young lives each year. Unless the expected growth in population of the developing world is matched by an increased commitment to provide adequate sanitation, these health problems are likely to expand.

While the greatest shortage of sanitation is found in rural areas, the need is most urgent in cities, because of the greater potential there for pathogen-tainted water to sicken people on a massive scale. This urban need poses a particular challenge, because the ranks of city dwellers will swell in the next century. In contrast to global population, which is projected to increase by 54 per cent over the next half-century, cities will see much greater growth—about 128 per cent. Developing country cities which failed to meet the sanitation needs of more than a half-billion residents in 1994, will be hard-pressed to service the more than 3 billion people who will be added to cities in the next 50 years.

Prospects for providing access to sanitation are dismal in the near to medium term. Just to keep from losing ground, the rate of provision of service to urban dwellers needs to more than double in Asia. In Africa, it would have to increase by 33 times. And to achieve full coverage by 2020, service provision would have to triple in Asia and increase by 46 times in Africa. Despite the attention focused on sanitation, governments have not demonstrated the will to meet this growing challenge.

17

Population Growth and Climate Change

Over the last half-century, carbon emissions from fossil fuel burning expanded at nearly twice the rate of population, boosting atmospheric concentrations of carbon dioxide, the principal greenhouse gas, by 30 per cent over pre-industrial levels. All major scientific bodies acknowledge the likelihood that climate change due to the buildup of greenhouse gases in the atmosphere is indeed under way. The 15 warmest years on record have all occurred since 1979, and 1998.

The destabilization of our climate threatens more intense heat waves, more severe droughts and floods, more destructive storms, and more extensive forest fires. The related shifts in rainfall and temperature may jeopardize food production, the Earth's biological diversity, and entire ecosystems, as well as human health by expanding the ranges of tropical diseases. Unless efforts to curb them are stepped up, carbon emissions will continue to grow faster than population over the next 50 years, driving the Earth's climate system into unchartered territory. The Intergovernmental Panel on Climate Change (IPCC) estimates that an eventual two-thirds reduction in global emissions is needed to avoid precariously high levels of atmospheric carbon dioxide concentrations.

The IPCC and the US Department of Energy (DOE) project that emissions from developing countries will nearly quadruple over the next half-century, while those from industrial nations will increase by 30 per cent. Although annual emissions from industrial countries are currently twice as high as from developing ones, the latter are on target to eclipse the industrial world by 2020.

Higher per capita emissions account for roughly 55 per cent of the increase in emissions projected for developing nations. Emissions per person are due to more than double from 0.51 tons of carbon per year in 2000—just one-fifth of the industrial level—to 1.14 tons in 2050. The remaining 45 per cent of emissions increases is due to population growth.

Fossil fuel use accounts for roughly three quarters of world carbon emissions. As a result, regional growth in carbon emissions tend to occur where economic activity, and related energy use, is projected to grow most rapidly. Emissions in China are projected to grow over three times faster than population in the next half-century, as emissions per person soar from 0.77 tons of carbon to 2.81 tons due to booming economy that is heavily reliant on coal and other carbon-rich energy sources. In Africa, in contrast, emissions per person are expected to scarcely change-growing from the current level of 0.33 tons in 2050, despite a threefold increase in total emissions.

The effects of population growth are most profound in countries where people are heavily emitters. For example, the 115 million people added to the population of the United States between 1950 and 1998—an increase of nearly 75 per cent in just 45 years—account for more than one-tenth of current global emissions. And the carbon emissions of the 75 million people who will be added to the US population in the next 50 years roughly equal the emissions of the 1.3 billion people who will be added to Africa during that period.

Deforestation and other land use changes account for the remainder of world carbon emissions. Forests have served as a sink for carbon throughout much of human history. In recent years, however, the world's forests have become net sources of atmospheric carbon, largely due to forest burning and clearing in the tropics. Six months of fires in Asia in 1997 and 1998 released more carbon than Western Europe emits from fossil fuel burning in an entire year. The carbon contribution from this source will likely increase in coming years as the burgeoning human population continues to cut down forests.

18

Action for Safe Motherhood

Countries vary enormously in terms of the situations and challenges they face and their capacity to address these. However, experience from around the world over the past decade has demonstrated that a number of features are common to successful efforts to address maternal mortality. Reducing maternal morality requires coordinated, long-term efforts. Actions are needed within families and communities, in society as a whole, in health systems, and at the level of national legislation and policy. Further, interactions among the interventions in these areas are critical to reducing maternal mortality and to building and supporting momentum for change.

LEGISLATIVE AND POLICY ACTIONS

Changes in legislation and policy are essential to ensure safe motherhood. Long-term political commitment is an essential prerequisite. When decision-makers at the highest levels are resolved to address maternal mortality, the resources needed will be mobilized and the essential policy decisions will be taken. Without this level of commitment over the long term, projects cannot become programmes and activities cannot be sustained.

A supportive social, economic, and legislative environment allows women to overcome the various obstacles that limit their access to health care, such as distance from their homes to appropriate health facilities, lack of transport and, more critically, financial and social barriers. Proper maternal health care is limited when women have to pay for services and essential drugs, and when they must bear substantial hidden costs such as time lost for housework, paid employment, food production, and child care. Legislation that supports women's access to care must be formulated to permit health workers at the periphery of the health system to perform specific life-saving functions. Failing this, only highly skilled health professionals, based largely in urban centres, can provide such care, and only women with sufficient money and the means to reach such centres can benefit from it.

With these objectives, careful review of national laws and policies is necessary, particularly in the following areas:

- **Family Planning.** Statutes that restrict women's access to family planning services (e.g. by requiring that a woman be married or that she should have her husband's approval) should be repealed. Policies must ensure that all couples and individuals have access to good-quality, voluntary, client-oriented, and confidential family planning information and to services that offer a wide choice of effective contraceptive methods. Policies should address regulatory, social, economic, and cultural factors that limit women's control over sexuality and reproduction, in order that pregnancies that are too early, too late, or too frequent may be avoided.

- **Adolescents and Children**. Polices and programmes should encourage later marriage and childbearing and an expansion of the economic and educational opportunities for girls and women. Promotion of good nutrition in childhood and adolescence, as well as supplementation if necessary during pregnancy, provides protection for both women and their future children. Policies should also enable adolescents to take responsibility for and protect their sexual and reproductive health, and facilitate their access to health information and services. All children, before they reach the age at which they become sexually active, need to be taught the risks of unprotected sex and helped to develop the skills needed to protect themselves from sexual coercion.

- **Barriers to Access**. Assigning health workers trained in midwifery to village-based health facilities can help over-come problems of distance and transport. Health workers should also be trained to deal sympathetically with women patients. Policies should support the provision of services at minimum cost; at the same time, health workers should have job security, be paid adequate wages, and be provided with sufficient supplies to do their jobs. Policies that will increase women's decision-making power, particularly in regard to their own health, are also essential.

- **Regulation of Practice**. Protocols and statutes aimed at providing both routine maternal care and referral facilities for obstetric complications at each level of the health system need to be developed. Responsibilities at each level of supervision, deployment of health care personnel, remuneration, and reporting procedures must be defined nationally. Development and promotion of education and training curricula are important, as is the setting of national norms and standards to govern the selection of trainees, trainers and supervisors.

- **Delegation of Authority.** Services should be decentralized so that facilities are available as close to people's homes as possible. Adequate supplies and equipment and trained staff should be available in all health facilities, particularly in rural and remote areas, together with written policies and protocols to guide service provision and to allow certain functions to be delegated to personnel at lower levels (when appropriately trained).

- **Abortion.** Availability of services for management of abortion complications and post-abortion care should be ensured by appropriate legislation. Where abortion is not prohibited by law, facilities for the safe termination of pregnancy should be made available. National policy can discourage unsafe abortion practices by promoting protection against unwanted pregnancy, and national health campaigns to publicize the risks of unsafe abortion and the need to recognize and seek treatment for abortion complications.

19

Safe Motherhood is a Human Rights Issue

The death of a woman during pregnancy or childbirth is not only a health issue but also a matter of social injustice. Of human rights currently acknowledged in national constitutions and in regional and international human rights treaties, many can be applied to safe motherhood. Many such treaties and conventions are based on the 1948 Declaration of Human Rights (1); they include the Convention on the Elimination of All Forms of Discrimination against Women (2), the Convention on the Rights of the Child (3), the European Convention for the Protection of Human Rights and Fundamental Freedoms (4), the American Convention on Human Rights (5), and the African Charter on Human and Peoples' Rights (6).

Human rights of relevance to safe motherhood can be grouped into the following four principal categories:

- **Rights relating to life, liberty and security of the person,** which require governments to ensure both access to appropriate health care during pregnancy and childbirth, and women's rights to decide whether, when, and how often to bear children. Governments must therefore address factors within the economic, legal, social, and health systems that deny women these fundamental rights.

- **Rights relating to the foundation of families and of family life**, which require governments to provide access to health services and other facilities that women need to establish families and to enjoy life within a family.

- **Rights relating to health care and the benefits of scientific progress**, including health information and education, which require governments to provide access to good sexual and reproductive health care with appropriate referral systems. The measures needed to ensure safe motherhood can be provided through primary health care irrespective of a country's level of economic development. Central to these rights is information on a range of reproductive health issues, including family planning, abortion, and sex education.

- **Rights relating to equality and nondiscrimination**, which require governments to provide access to services such as education and health care without discriminatory grounds such as sex, marital status, age, and socioeconomic class. Discriminatory policies include requirements for a woman to obtain the consent of her husband for particular health care interventions, requirements for parental authorization which have a differential impact on girls, and laws the criminalize medical procedures that only women need. Governments are in violation of their obligations when they fail to implement laws that effectively protect women's interests or to allocate health resources to meet women's particular need for safe pregnancy and childbirth.

The actions that governments need to take to promote safe motherhood as a human right fall into three groups:

- **Reform of laws** that prevent women from attaining the highest possible levels of health and nutrition needed for safe pregnancy and childbirth and that inhibit access to reproductive health information and services such as laws requiring women in need of health care to seek the authorization of husbands or other family members first.

- **Implementation of laws** that foster women's rights to good health and nutrition and that protect women's health interests such as laws that prohibit child marriage, female genital mutilation, rape, and sexual abuse. Every effort should be made to implement laws that encourage the healthy timing of births, such as those that support the education of girls, set a minimum age for marriage, and ensure women's access to essential health care.

- **Application of human rights** in national legislation and policy to advance safe motherhood.

20

What is Known About Reducing Maternal Mortality?

Historical records demonstrate the significant improvements that can be achieved when key interventions are in place. Reductions in maternal mortality took place in Sweden during the 1800s, for example, as a result of a national policy favouring professional midwifery care for all births, coupled with establishment of standards for quality of care. By the beginning of the 20th century, maternal mortality in Sweden was the lowest around 230 per 1,00,000 live births compared with over 500 per 1,00,000 in the mid-1980s. In Denmark, Japan, Netherlands, and Norway, similar strategies produced comparable results. In England and Wales, significant reductions in maternal mortality were not apparent until the 1930s; at the national level, political commitment to the strategy was achieved only slowly and the introduction of professional midwifery was correspondingly delayed. In every case, however, the key to these improvements was the institution of fully professional maternity care.

In the USA, where strategy focused on hospital delivery by doctors, maternal mortality remained high because it proved difficult to establish adequate regulatory frameworks and mechanisms to ensure quality of care. In 1930, the maternal mortality ratio in the USA was still 700 per 1,00,000 live births compared with 430 in England and Wales.

More recently, India witnessed significant reductions in maternal mortality in a relatively short period. From a level of over 1500 per 1,00,000 live births in 1940-45, maternal mortality fell to 555 per 1,00,000 in 1950-55, 239 per 1,00,000 within 10 years, 95 per 1,00,000 by 1980. The figure is now 30 per 1,00,000. These improvements followed the introduction of a system of health facilities around the country allied to an expansion of midwifery skills and the spread of family planning. During the 1950s most births in India took place at home with the assistance of untrained birth attendants. By the end of the 1980s over 85 per cent of all births were attended by trained personnel.

Similar evidence of the effectiveness of health care interventions is available from China, Cuba, and Malaysia. These countries established community-based maternal health care systems comprising prenatal, delivery, and postpartum care and a system of referral to a higher level of care in the event of obstetric complications.

What these examples clearly demonstrate is that a country's overall economic wealth is not in itself the most important determinant of maternal mortality. There are numerous other examples of countries with modest levels of GNP which have achieved low maternal mortality.

21

Food First

By the time this day is over, about 40,000 human beings—mostly children—will have died from hunger, malnutrition and related causes. Today and every day the deaths will mount, reaching an annual toll of 13 to 18 million. Few of these people will have been caught up in famine or other emergencies. Most will have suffered from a 'silent' assault—the kind that seldom makes the headlines, but which claims its victims just as relentlessly.

It is intolerable that such deprivation and suffering should be allowed to exist in a world of potential food plenty. Having enough food is fundamental to all else. At the most basic level, this may entail humanitarian relief to assist people in emergency situations. In the transition from relief to development, however, we must look at systems for ensuring that societies have the capacity to produce or purchase the food they need and that it is accessible to all.

Sustainable food security fuses the goals of household food security and sustainable agriculture; it requires both. It requires looking not only at the aggregate supply of food, but also at the distribution of income and land, and at other issues: Do people have enough income to buy food? Enough land to grow their own food? Does the food distribution system deliver food where it is needed? How much food is wasted due to inadequate distribution systems? What are the implications of trends in population growth for future food needs? What is the status of women in society, and what opportunities do women have to alter rapid population growth rates? What is being done to regenerate the resource base for food production? These questions need to be asked and answered in every country.

The challenge of sustainable food security is immense, and it is growing. One billion people—20 per cent of the global population—are too poor to obtain enough food to sustain normal work. Half a billion are too poor to obtain the food needed for healthy growth of children and minimal activity of adults. Today's failure to feed people, however, may be but a prologue to a much larger failure in the future. Given likely population increases, world food output must triple over the next 50 years if the world's people are to have a nutritionally adequate diet. It will be difficult enough to achieve this expansion under favourable circumstances, and conditions may be far from favourable.

For example, according to recent estimates an area of about 1.2 billion hectares—the size of China and India combined—has experienced moderate to extreme soil deterioration since World War II as a result of human activities. Over three-fourths of that deterioration has occurred in the developing regions from causes such as overgrazing, deforestation, land clearing, unsound agricultural practices and increased soil salinity and waterlogging, largely from irrigation. Other environmental threats to the agricultural resource base include loss of water and genetic resources, adverse effects of pesticides and climate change, both local and global.

At the most aggregate level, the required increase in food production could be met if production grew at the historic average, that is, at the two per cent per annum rate achieved over the past half-century. But is this realistic? To produce three times more calories, all the land currently under cultivation around the world would, within 50 years, have to attain levels of productivity as high as those exhibited by the very best cropland today.

To this challenge add the possibility of diminished returns from the technological, energy and other inputs that have made agriculture so successful. Some experts believe that most of the potential for increased output of cereals—from improved plant varieties, from increased use of pesticides and fertilizers and from expanding the area under irrigation—has already been captured.

Viewed from this perspective, the goal of achieving sustainable food security in the decades ahead emerges as one of the greatest challenges humanity has ever faced. Agricultural output must be tripled, and people must have the income to buy the food they need. The erosion of the resource base must be halted and then reversed. Failure on any of these fronts will yield unprecedented human suffering.

What will it take to achieve sustainable food security? Obviously, the effort will have to be immense, both in size and complexity. Outlined below are a few simple (but no easy) steps that are absolutely essential elements of serious effort.

First, as citizens of the world, we must all come to see sustainable food security as a fundamental aspect of global peace and human security. This goes well beyond merely denouncing the use of food as a weapon.

Second, we must adopt concrete international goals, such as reducing world hunger by half over the next 10 years. We will never achieve the goal of sustainable food security unless we aim at specific milestones, and assess rigorously our progress in moving toward them.

Third, we must forge a true global partnership, a compact for sustainable food security. All countries—rich and poor—have important roles and responsibilities. There must be reciprocal responsibilities among nations, not one-way transfers.

Fourth, we must see deterioration of the agricultural resource base—terrestrial, aquatic and climatic—for what it is: a major threat to development and a major source of economic loss. Farmers are the largest group of environmental decision-makers in the world. We must ensure that they have the means to make sustainable development a reality where it counts–in the fields and fisheries.

Fifth, we must empower the people who work the land and who keep it productive. They are in the best position to decide the most appropriate ways to graft new technology onto their own traditional knowledge of seed selection, plant protection and nutrient-cycling. Special emphasis should be given to the role of women, the main providers for two-thirds of the poorest households in the developing world, as well as the producers of 60 per cent of all food grown and consumed locally.

Sixth, we must build the capacities of developing countries, both in government and in civil society. Capacity-building means empowerment for self-reliance. It means strengthening national capacities, both inside and outside government. This is essential for recognition and analysis of problems, for decision-making on courses of action and for management of systems and processes.

Seventh, not only must we build capacity in developing countries, we must also create linkages among researchers in industrial and developing countries. This will help minimize the time lag between discovery and practical utilization. In addition, analysts from various countries must work together to examine future food security issues with different scenarios of population growth, agricultural productivity, markets and trade, climate change, loss of soil and bio-diversity and, last but not least, political instability, in order to devise options for rational choices.

We know a good deal about how to rid the world of the scourge of hunger, and how to begin to move toward sustainable food security on a global basis. We know that economic growth and prosperity are necessary, though not sufficient, conditions for eradicating hunger. We also know that development efforts must encompass not only food production, but also socio-economic factors, including sustainable livelihoods for poor families, the implications of population growth rates, the status of women and girls and so forth. We also know that good words are not enough. Now more than ever before it is crucial that we marshal the political will to achieve our goals.

22

Population—Male Friendly Approach to Family. Planning

Men are more like to be in favour of family planning and to use a method themselves if programmes and services are provided through 'men only' clinics, and educational programmes are conducted men to men. This has been demonstrated in several studies and by the popularity of such approaches when they have been introduced to control population.

Human beings will resist changes which threaten their security. Very often in the field of family planning, programme objectives contain worlds or slogans which threaten men. The men end up rejecting programmes which, if presented in different ways, would gain their full support and participation.

Programmes which empower women to deny men their human rights and freedoms are not male friendly. Instead, those working in family planning should encourage men to accept, respect and promote the sexual and reproductive rights and freedoms of women. Families thrive on sharing, and programmes of change could usefully focus on persuading men to become more involved in reproductive health issues and in sharing the burden of family planning with their wives or partners.

Malefriendly approaches should address the fears of men. For example, there is a deep-rooted fear that contraception endows women with too much freedom and so reduces a husband's span of control over a wife's sexuality. Some men believe that contraception causes unfaithfulness and that continuous childbearing places unfaithfulness under control.

While it is essential to promote programmes which empower women to exercise control over their fertility, such programmes can improve their chances of success if implemented alongside educational programmes which help men to understand the rationale and need for them to be sensitive and responsive to the needs of women, and why sexual and reproductive health decisions should be the joint responsibility of men and women.

The concept of rights can imply militancy, so care must be taken if statements of programme objectives and goals are phrased in terms of rights. A process of change has to be courted through education and persuasion. The more men are reminded of women's reproductive health rights without proper explanation, the more they will resist positive change.

Malefriendly and negotiated approaches can speed up the move towards gender equality in matters of planned parenthood. Promoting spousal communication will encourage mutual understanding between husbands and wives on sexual and reproductive health decisions and practices. Family life education programmes which promote respectful and harmonious partnership between males and females, young and old can be a good starting point. As well as educating men about the benefits of sharing more equally in family life, such programmes should help family members understand their sexuality and inform them how to protect themselves from unwanted pregnancies, sexually transmitted diseases and other sexual and reproductive health problems and population.

Malefriendly approaches can go a long way to moderate societal and cultural barriers that prevent men take joint decisions with women on family planning and sexual and reproductive health, and sharing the responsibility with them. And they can achieve far better results than programmes which threaten men's security and which diminish their feeling of masculinity.

23

Has the Tide Turned? Successes in Family Planning

Good news from the population front. While during the last decades since 1950 the world population kept growing at an ever faster pace, the yearly increases now seem to be stagnating at around 86 to 90 million. Whereas experts had expected yearly increases of up to 100 million only a short while ago, the actual figures have now turned out to be considerably lower. This means that world population growth may have reached its peak in the 1980s, and that we are now entering a phase of slower growth which, eventually, may lead to a consolidation of world population.

The main reason for the decline in growth rates is the falling fertility of women, especially in developing countries. In Bangladesh, for instance, the number of children per mother has dropped from 6.5 to 3.5 within two decades—a success of family planning which few experts would have thought possible only a few years ago. In spite of all obstacles posed by culture, religion or lacking access to family planning methods, the number of couples practising family planning in developing countries has risen from 14 to 57 per cent during the last 30 years. Even in Sub-Saharan Africa, which still has the highest birth rates of all developing regions, the number of children per woman dropped from 6.7 in 1980 to 6.2 now. Every second woman in Africa says she does not want to have additional children.

The latest figures on population growth will be welcomed by all who fear that the rapid population increases of the last decades may jeopardize the advances made during the same time in social and economic development. But it is much too early to give the all clear signal. One in four pregnancies is still neither planned nor wanted. And 350 million couples still have no access to modern family planning methods. Powerful traditions in African, Asian and Latin American societies, but also the orthodox views of the Pope and Islamic fundamentalists still stand in the way of effective family planning. No matter how quickly these obstacles will be overcome, world population will rise from its present 5.7 billion to at least 8 billion by the middle of next century. But it makes a big difference whether world population will be at the high or the low end of prognosticated levels—whether there will be 8 or 12 billion people living of the scarce resources and fragile eco-system of our planet.

The Cairo Plan of Action which was adopted at the last World Population Conference focusses on meeting the unmet need in family planning services by the year 2015. Fertility will drop by an average of 20 per cent if all women who would like to apply contraception are actually given the physical means to do so. In countries of Africa and South Asia, where contraceptives are still relatively difficult to obtain, the effect of general availability of family planning methods would even be more dramatic.

The key to increasing the use of contraceptives is communication. Information about family planning can be conveyed either through individual communicators in family planning projects or through the mass media. Soap operas on this subject have been very successful in sensitizing large parts of the population in Latin America and Asia. Sexual instruction for youths is another important way to spread the knowledge on family planning.

In any case, the current trends are encouraging. Most governments around the world are now convinced that population growth cannot be allowed to go unchecked. The subject of family planning is no longer a taboo. And all those who always say that world conferences like the one in Cairo do not achieve anything should have a good look at the latest figures. Had it not been for the hard and persistent work of UNFPA, IPPF and other organizations the tide may not have turned as quickly as it did. In the Global village in which we all live these days, the word seems to have spread that smaller families are better for the individual and for the world as a whole. More communication on the subject is needed if the present success is to be maintained.

24

Population Growth—Facts and Figures

The World-wide rate of population growth has been essentially the same since 1975, at about 1.7 per cent a year. Fertility is actually going down slightly, from 3.8 in 1975-80 to 3.3 in 1990-95. Because of past growth, however, the number of people added each year is still rising. In 1975, the annual addition was about 72 million. In 1992 it was 93 million. It will peak between 1995 and 2000, at about 98 million annually.

Rapid population growth is therefore still the dominant feature of global demographics, and will continue to be so for atleast the next 30 years. The 1993 global population of 5.57 billion is projected to increase to 6.25 billion in 2000, 8.5 billion in 2025 and 10 billion in 2050; significant growth will probably continue until about 2150 and a level of about 11.6 billion.

The developing countries' proportion of this increase grew from 77 per cent in 1950 to 93 per cent in 1990; between now and the end of the century it will be 95 per cent. Africa and South Asia alone account for 53 per cent.

Asia's population in mid-1993 was 3.3 billion. By 2025, Asia will have 4.9 billion people, equal to the whole of world population in 1986; Africa (700 million) will have 1.6 billion; Latin America (466 million) will have 700 million people.

This overall picture conceals wide variations from country to country and region to region. For example:

— Annual growth 1990-95 is estimated at 3.0 per cent for Africa, with Asia at 1.9 per cent and Latin America 2.1 per cent. By and large the fastest rates of growth are in the poorest countries.

— The 47 Countries officially designated by the Demographers as 'least developed' accounted for 7 per cent of global increase in 1950, but 13 per cent by 1990.

— Life expectancy has increased by 30 years in East Asia over the last four decades, as against 15 years in Africa, which has 30 of the 47 'least developed' countries.

— Fertility has fallen by 60 per cent in East Asia in the same period, but by only 25 per cent in South Asia and hardly at all in Africa.

— Maternal mortality has been halved in East Asia, but remains virtually unchanged in South Asia and Africa.

Among developing countries, the lowest growth rates are in East Asia and the Caribbean (1.3 per cent). East Asia's growth rates largely reflect the situation in China, which is 85 per cent of the region. Central and South America, South-East and South Asia and Southern Africa lie between 2 and 2.5 per cent; North Africa and West Asia between 2.5 and 3; and the rest of Africa over 3 per cent.

The biggest variation of all has grown up between the industrialized countries of Europe and North America, and the rest of the world. In the industrialized countries population growth has slowed or stopped altogether, and fertility is at or below replacement level. Their populations increased by 43 per cent between 1950 and 1990, compared with 162 per cent among the least developed countries and 140 per cent in the other developing countries. This variation will deepen: the populations of Europe and sub-Saharan Africa, roughly the same in 1985 at about 480 million, will be 500 million and 1500 million respectively by 2025.

Asia has 59 per cent of world population, Latin America 9 per cent and Africa 12 per cent. Africa's share is projected to go up to 19 per cent by 2025, while proportions in the other regions remain about the same. Within Asia the proportions are changing: China, now 37 per cent of Asia's population, will be 31 per cent by 2025; India will go from 27 per cent to 29 per cent.

25

Our Crowded World

It has been 40 years since India first began braking runaway population growth. The programmes have largely been failures, including the widely reviled sterilization campaign of the early '70s that still haunts old men and sends them scurrying at the sight of an unfamiliar face.

By the end of this decade, India's Chaotic cities and countless villages are expected to be home for one in every six people on earth.

By early next century, if the projections are correct, more people will live in Indian in any other country, including China, Sparse resources will be stretched among even more desperately poor people. Pressure on forests, rivers and agricultural land already under siege will mount.

Growing number of experts in the Third World believe that population control programmes will never work. In China, despite draconian measures to restrict each family to one child, population-control programmes are failing.

Even in Indonesia, touted as one of the world's success stories, the health of thousands of women is jeopardized by contraceptive devices. It is time for hormonal implants in their arms to be removed, but no one has kept track of where they live. There is also evidence many were forced by the military to take part in birth-control programmes.

Although there has been some success in getting women around the world to have fewer children, huge numbers are just now entering their reproductive stage.

The United Nations estimates six billion by 1998. By the year 2050, those numbers to almost double to 10 billion, and perhaps—if its most optimistic projections are true—level off at 11.6 billion a century later and then begin to fall.

The UN has warned that much depends on action taken during the next decade, saying a delay could mean upto four billion extra people—which was the world's population in 1975—by 2050, and upto 20.7 billion a century later.

But it isn't all bad news. Population growth has slowed in countries where the standard of living has improved and where women have access to education and jobs.

In Thailand, for example, female literacy is now at 90 per cent, and the fertility rate has declined significantly.

If people have jobs, if women can read, the population goes down. It is difficult to tell people, especially in a democracy, what they must do about something as personal as birth control. The rich countries, where population growth is much slower, have become increasingly concerned about the explosion in the Third World.

26

The Good News about Population Growth

Global population is growing at an ominous pace. Yet new opportunities, if they are seized, along with changes in government policies, could help solve the population problem within two generations. Three facts of the impact of population growth on economic and human development are:

- The countries of the developing world already contain three quarters of humanity and will soon be home to nine of every 10 people on Earth.
- With but a small fraction of the world's GNP, a tiny percentage of its scientists, the lion's share of its debt and nearly all of its abject poor, these countries have been ill-equipped to absorb

the dramatic increases in human numbers that, despite the steadily declining rate of global population growth, has occurred since the end of World War-II.

- Within the next 60 years, between three and seven billion more people will be added to the population of the developing world. Assuming they can sustain such increases, developing countries will double or triple in size before their populations are stabilized a century or more from now. If they cannot, and population size outstrips the resources available to support it, population growth will be slowed faster and sooner, on nature's grim terms.

The conventional wisdom is that because rapid population growth lowers per capita expenditures on education, per capita access to renewable natural resources, and per capita savings rates, it retards economic and social development. But the problem goes beyond this conventional wisdom. There is a lethal synergy that exists in dozens of developing countries between the sheer speed of population growth, on the one hand, and inappropriate government policies that magnify its negative effects, on the other. The former is suggested by the fact that the populations of most developing countries are projected to double in size in 30 years or less. The latter is evident in policies that have prevented many developing countries from either slowing such growth or accommodating it gracefully.

It would stretch the capacities of even the most prosperous countries if they had to accommodate the kind of population growth expected in regions including sub-Saharan Africa and South Asia. Without the benefit of prosperity, the indispensable requirement will be for governments to formulate policies that will alleviate rather than exacerabate the economic and social effects of rapid population growth. But as examples from around the developing world illustrate, such policies are in short supply. In Africa, food supplies are inadequate partly because of a pervasive urban bias that leaves farmers with few incentives to produce. In dozens of command economies, housing for low-income families is limited because of anachronistic rent control laws, which have discouraged private developers from building new residential housing units. In other developing countries, significant resources that could be invested in education are diverted for military use. In few of these countries is rapid population growth the main factor retarding economic growth. But in most, such growth has exacerbated the negative effects of short-sighted policies and it will likely do so to a greater degree in the future, for reasons ranging from inexperience in self-government to political opportunism to bureaucratic inaptitude.

High political and institutional barriers thus separate what can be done to mitigate the effects of rapid population growth from what is likely to be done in all to many countries. That's the bad news one has to face as they grapple with the problem of rapid population growth. The good news is that where such barriers have been lowered by far-sighted governments, the results have been hopeful and in some cases dramatic. Sustained high agricultural growth has taken place, in a number of countries—where constraints on small-scale agriculture have been removed. Significant progress has also been achieved by some of the thousands of non-governmental organizations (NGOs) that are playing an increasingly important role in solving population-related problems at the local level in developing countries around the world.

In Bangladesh, meanwhile, the innovative work of two other well-know NGOs—the Grameen Bank and the Bangladesh Rural Advancement Committee—has helped to unleash the productive potential of scores of thousands of poor women, with clear implications not only for economic development but also for fertility reduction. Researchers say the 'micro-enterprise' loans given by the banks have changed attitudes towards childbearing by empowering women, raising the 'opportunity costs' of having large families and producing a greater degree of parity in marriage relationships. Creating a sense of a future that extends beyond mere day-to-day survival has changed the context for decisions about family size.

Nor is the work of NGOs the only hopeful development weighing in the balance against unprecedented increases in population that are all but certain to occur over the next few decades. As the 21st century approaches there is a heartening convergence of factors that augur well for stabilizing global population, sooner perhaps than experts would have thought possible even a decade ago.

The most consequential factor many be the growing desire on the part of men and women around the world for access to family planning services. Millions more, including sexually active young people and couples discouraged from practising family planning by the poor quality of existing services, could be reached by well-run family planning programmes, especially those sensitive to the reproductive health needs of women. Family planning agencies are confident that, in the process of satisfying the existing demand for family planning services, they can create new demand by improving the quality of services and legitimizing the small-family model .

Across the institutional spectrum, from national governments in rich and poor nations alike, to giant multi-lateral institutions there is a growing recognition that the future will pose far greater challenges to the human race if rates of population growth are not slowed further. Significantly, that conclusion has recently been endorsed by a growing number of natural scientists who now warn that, without global efforts to slow population growth, science and technology may not be able to redeem the future from want and hunger. One can predict that if current population and consumption trends continue, 'science and technology may not be able to prevent either irreversible degradation of the environment or continued poverty for much of the world'.

Rates of contraceptive use among men and women, who in every other respect regard themselves as faithful Catholics, are as high as or higher than those of non-Catholics. The lowest birthrates and highest contraceptive use rates on record have been achieved in Catholic World, where abortion is also widely favoured as a back-up in case of contraceptive failure. Similar attitudes are found in the Islamic World, where rapid population growth has prompted theologians to accent a more permissive side of their theology with respect to the use of modern contraceptives. The results have been strong clerical support for family planning programmes.

Beyond the diminished obstacles to progress is the increased opportunity for progress that has been created by the end of the cold war. Freed from the necessity of concentrating on geostrategic threats to peace, policy makers now have the luxury of turning their attention to the global forces that impinge on the peace and prosperity of nations, including the pressure population growth is placing on economic development, food supplies and the natural environment. Worried that such pressures could destabilize the governments of poor nations, prompt interstate conflict over scarce resources, and spur disruptive movements of populations into urban areas or across national frontiers, Western analysts are even now thinking of ways to retool foreign policy to cope with the proliferating number of local threats. On crucial task will be to monitor environmental and economic conditions around the developing world and to provide early warning of regional conflicts. More difficult to implement will be longer-range approaches, including a refashioning of the international trading system to provide more equity to poor nations.

If political leaders are willing and able to capitalize on the opportunity provided by the coming together of this extra-ordinary constellation of circumstances, the population problem could be solved within two generations. If they are not, providing for the welfare of humanity in tne century ahead will be more difficult; perhaps, in some of the world's poorest regions, it will prove impossible.

27

Food for the Billions

Will there be enough food to feed 8 billion people who will live on earth in 25 years' time? Surprisingly few people, at least in the industrial countries, seems to be overly concerned with this question. Whereas the world conferences on the environment, on women, human rights or social issues which were held in recent years were preceded and accompanied by intensive public debate, food does not seem to be a burning issue. Don't we have mountains of surplus food, people ask. Do we not have to pay our farmers to leave their land idle in order not to add to the glut on the world markets? And hasn't the Green Revolution ended famine even in countries like India which used to be a synonym for hungry people? So where is the problem?

The advance made in agricultural production since beginning against a background of imminent crisis are indeed remarkable. In only 20 years, yields of major crops like rice, maize and wheat in developing countries went up by 80 per cent, outpacing even the rapid increase in population. But this growth in yields has slowed down in recent years, and the aim of 'food for all' is once again becoming elusive. About 800 million people still do not have access to enough food to meet their basic daily needs, nearly 200 million children suffer from protein and energy deficiencies, 88 countries—44 of them in Africa—have a deficit in food production.

Every one wants to increase food security. The definition is that 'food be available at all times, that all persons have means of access to it, that it be nutritionally adequate in terms of quantity, quality and variety, and that it be acceptable within the given culture'. To achieve this goal, more food must be produced—much more, because we must not only adequately feed the 5.8 billion people already on earth, but also the additional two billion who will be added to world population in the next 25 years. Critics argue that the problem is not one of production alone, but one of poverty elimination. People are not hungry because there is no food, but because they have no money to buy it, these critics say. Available resources must be better distributed to end hunger in the world.

However, even if we succeed to eliminate poverty in the next few decades—a feat which appears highly unlikely—there would still be the need to boost production, because with rising incomes people also want to eat more and better food including meat. As can already be observed in the countries of East Asia, the newly acquired wealth leads to higher consumption levels which puts additional strains on available resources are getting scarcer. Agricultural lands are being degraded at alarming speed by erosion, salinity, desertification or disappear altogether due to urban or infrastructure development. It has been estimated that 40 per cent of productive land now has diminished capacity to supply benefits to humanity due to direct human impacts of land use. Water for agricultural purposes is getting scarcer almost everywhere, and there are hardly and land reserves to be brought into production to widen the agricultural base.

In this situation, there is no alternative to increasing and improving production from the existing land area. This can only be done through research which finds the best varieties which will bring the highest yields at the lowest cost to the environment. Sustainable agriculture is the key notion one that maintains bio-diversity, uses as little chemical inputs as possible and does not over exploit water and soil resources.

In recent years, agricultural research has been neglected partly because of the erroneous belief that with mountains of meat and lakes of milk further production increases were not desirable. Since global grain production has stagnated and world stocks have reached an alarmingly low level last year, there has been a noticeable change of mind. To raise the awareness among governments around the world that promotion of agriculture is urgent if hunger is to be avoided in the next century.

Important work is already being done by the international agricultural research institutes which promoted the Green Revolution in the sixties and seventies and are now again in the forefront of finding solutions to the daunting task of feeding 8 billion people by the year 2020. The International Rice Research Institute (IRRI) in the Philippines, the Maize and Wheat Research Institute (CIMMYT) in Mexico or institutes like ICARDA in Syria and ICRISAT in India which work on agriculture in semi-arid and dry areas, are all seeking solutions to the problem of raising production while at the same time preserving the environment. These institutions as well as national agricultural research institutions need all the support from the public and, of course, appropriate funding, to help them accomplish their task.

The scientists are optimistic that they can develop the varieties and farming systems which will allow mankind to feed everyone on earth well into the next century. But the task is not for the scientists alone. An economic and political order must also be in place which makes it possible to eradicate poverty and allow everyone to enjoy the benefits that science can offer. Feeding the billions is, therefore, not only a scientific, but first and foremost a political.

28

Fertility Rates: The Decline is Stalling

During the 1970's one of the population trends was the reduction in the total fertility rate in several key countries, including the world's two largest nations—China and India (the fertility rate measures the average number of children born to women in their childbearing years). In China, the rate dropped precipitously, from 6.4 children per woman in 1968 to 2.2 in 1980. In India, the decline was more modest, but still significant: from 5.8 children per woman between 1966 and 1971 to 4.8 children between 1976 and 1981.

These trends helped slow the rate of world population growth from 2.1 per cent between 1965 and 1970 to 1.7 per cent between 1975 and 1980. At that point, however, the decline in the number of children that women were having in these two population giants stalled.

In China, despite the most aggressive and least democratic population control programme in the world, the fertility rate remained around 2.5 throughout much of the 1980s as couples continued to want to marry young and to have two or more children. In India, the overzealous promotion of family planning by the ruling Congress Party through 1977 apparently backfired after the party's defeat, and progress toward lower birth rates ran out of steam.

One important lesson from these experiences is that governments must do more than just supply contraceptives; they need to lower the demand for children by making fundamental changes that improve women's lives and increase their access to and control over money, credit, and other resources.

Many countries still register fertility rates above replacement level (See Table), which is generally 2.1 children per woman or basically two children per couple. The total fertility rate for the world as a whole in 1995 was 3.3, ranging from 1.8 in more developed nations to 4.4 in less developed ones (excluding China). In a number of countries, such as Brazil, Egypt, Indonesia, Mexico, and Thailand, fertility rates have been dropping as they did in the 1970s in China and India. At the same time, many developing countries have not yet entered the demographic transition.

The demographic transition occurs when both birth rates and death rates in a country drop from historically high levels to low ones that translate into a stable population—one that merely replaces itself with each new generation. Traditionally, although not always, death rates have declined first, following the spread of sanitation and improved health care overall. Rapid population growth often follows this first phase of the demographic transition, as the gap between fertility and mortality rates widens for a time. Eventually, however, fertility rates fall too.

Population Size, Fertility Rate, and Doubling Time, 20 Largest Countries, 1995

Country	*Fertility Population (millions)*	*Rate (average number of children per woman)*	*Doubling Time (years)*
Italy	58	1.3	3466
Germany	81	1.4	*
Japan	125	1.5	217
United Kingdom	58	1.8	267
France	58	1.8	169
Russia	149	1.7	990
United States	258	2.0	92
China	1178	1.9	60
Thailand	57	2.4	49
Indonesia	188	3.0	42
Brazil	152	3.6	46
Turkey	61	3.6	32
Mexico	90	3.4	13
India	97	3.9	34
Vietnam	72	4.0	31
Philippines	5	4.1	28
Egypt	8	4.6	30
Pakistan	122	6.7	23
Iran	3	6.6	20
Nigeria	5	6.6	23

Source: Population Reference Bureau, 1995 World Population Data Sheet (Washington, DC: 1995).

At the moment, they remain high in a number of countries. The reasons include unequal rights and opportunities for women, as well as inadequate access to birth control. Whatever the reason, the effect is the same: 67 countries, home to 17 per cent of the world population, are at best in the early stages of a transition to low fertility rates. Most of them are in Africa and South Asia, and their populations are likely to double in 20 to 25 years.

This is leading to a two-tiered demographic world that is every bit as worrying as the world of economic haves and have-nots. Countries such as Nigeria and Pakistan are finding it harder to keep up with the demand for food, health care, jobs, housing, and education than countries that are in the middle of the demographic transition.

Even when a country does reach replacement-level fertility, its population can continue growing for decades. There is a built-in momentum created by all the people who have yet to enter their childbearing years. Indeed, the decline in the world's population growth rate stalled in the 1980s in part because even in China, India, and other countries where fertility rates had been dropping, large number of people who had been born in the 1960s reached childbearing age. So even if couples had two or three children instead of five or six, as their parents did, the population would grow substantially.

For the world as a whole, even if replacement-level fertility had been achieved in 1990, the population would continue to grow until it reached 8.4 billion in 2150 because of all the young people already alive. This built-in momentum obviously limits how quickly any country can stop population growth. Nevertheless, reaching replacement level fertility is an all-important first step. The 67 countries that have not yet begun the demographic transition—nations in which invariably the government believes fertility levels are too high—could move in the right direction by providing the contraceptive and health care services that would help couples have only the number of children they desire.

29

The Population Challenge

During the last half-century world population has more than doubled, climbing from 2.5 billion in 1950 to 5.9 billion in 1998. Those of us born before 1950 are members of the first generation to witness a doubling of world population. Stated otherwise, there has been more growth in population since 1950 than during the 4 million years since our early ancestors first stood upright.

This unprecedented surge in population combined with rising individual consumption, is pushing our claims on the planet beyond its natural limits. Water tables area falling on every continent as demand exceeds the sustainable yield of aquifers. Eventual aquifer depletion will bring irrigation cutbacks and shrinking harvests. Our growing appetite for seafood has pushed oceanic fisheries to their limits and beyond. Collapsing fisheries tell us we can go no further. The Earth's temperature is rising, promising changes in climate that we cannot even anticipate. We are triggering the greatest extinction of plant and animal species since the dinosaurs disappeared. As our numbers go up, their numbers go down.

These effects of population growth are relatively recent, but assertions that population growth could affect human welfare are not. In 1798 Thomas Malthus, a British clergyman and intellectual, warned in his famous piece, *An Essay on the Principles of Population*, of the tendency for population to grow exponentially while food supply grew arithmetically. He saw a world where human numbers would continually press against available food supplies.

During the 200 years since Malthus issued his warning, famine has visited countries as diverse as Ireland and India, Ethiopia and China. Indeed, despite the near-tripling of the world grain harvest since 1950 the hungry and malnourished in 1998 number an estimated 840 million—nearly as many people as lived in the world when Malthus penned his essay.

But the nature of famine has changed. Whereas it was once geographically defined by areas of poor harvests, today famine is economically defined by low incomes in those segments of society that lack the purchasing power to buy enough food. Famine concentrated among the poor is less visible than the more traditional version but is no less real.

In addition to checks imposed by food shortages, there is evidence that other checks on population growth are now emerging, such as new infectious diseases, including AIDS, Ethnic conflicts within societies, such as Rwanada and the Sudan, are also taking a growing toll. Water shortages on a scale that would deprive people of enough water to produce food could undermine governments.

The evidence gathered here indicates that the rapid population growth prevailing in a majority of the world's countries is not going to continue much longer. Either countries will get their act together, shifting quickly to smaller families, or death rates will rise from one or more of the stresses just mentioned. As human demands press against more and more of the Earth's limits, the questions is not whether population growth will slow, but how. Will it be because countries do it humanely by shifting quickly to smaller families? Or because they fail to do so, and nature ruthlessly imposes its own constraints? In a world facing many challenges as it prepares to enter the next century, this may be the most challenging of all.

Estimates of future numbers are based on the latest United Nations population projections, using their medium level figures. Under this scenario, world population will grow from 6.1 billion in 2000 to 9.4 billion in 2050—a gain of 3.3 billion. The other two UN projections put global population in 2050 as high as 11.2 billion or as low as 7.7 billion. While the medium scenario is judged by the UN demographers as the one most likely to materialize, it is not an inevitable population path for the next century. Indeed, because the projections are based exclusively on demographic assumptions and do not take into account the environmental limits to carrying capacity, they should be viewed as a first pass rather than the final word on estimates of future population.

We use the medium-level projections to give an idea of the strain this 'most likely' outcome would place on ecosystems and governments, and the urgent need to break from the business-as-usual scenario. The mid-level projected growth in population of 3.3 billion by 2050 is very close to the growth that will have occurred between 1950 and 2000, some 3.6 billion. But there is one difference.

During the half-century now ending, the growth occurred in both industrial and developing countries. During the next half-century, the entire burden of the projected increase of 3.3 billion will be in developing countries, many of which are hard-pressed to satisfy even existing demands on resources. In fact, the population of the industrial world is expected to decline slightly.

The annual rate of world population growth reached its historical high in 1964 at 2.2 per cent. Since then, it has been slowly declining, dropping to 1.4 per cent in 1998. Despite the failing rate of growth the number of people aged each year increased from 72 million in 1964 to the all-time peak of 87 million in 1990. Since then the annual addition has also declined, falling to 80 million in 1997, where it is projected to remain for the next two decades before starting to decline.

The population projections for individual countries vary more widely than at any time in history. At mid-century populations were growing everywhere, but today they have stabilized in some 32 countries, while they continue to expand in some countries at 3 per cent or more a year. Indeed, the world can be divided demographically into two camps: countries that have achieved population stability or are well on the way to doing so, and those that have not.

With the exception of Japan, all the nations in the first camp are in Europe. And all are industrial countries. The populations of some countries, including Russia, Japan, and Germany, are actually projected to decline somewhat over the next half-century. In addition to the 32 countries, containing 12 per cent of world population, that have stabilized their populations, in another 39 countries fertility has dropped to replacement level [roughly two children per couple] or below. Among the countries in this category are China and the

United States the first and third largest countries, which together contain 26 per cent of the world's people.

Although fertility in these 39 countries has fallen below replacement level, their populations have not yet stabilized because there is a disproportionately large number of young people moving into the reproductive age group. Thus even if they hold their fertility at replacement level, population may continue to grow for several decades before it stabilizes. It was this realization that led China nearly 20 years ago to shift its goal from a two-child to a one-child family. Leaders in Beijing realized that if they did not do this they would be faced with adding the equivalent of another India to their population—a development they considered potentially disastrous for their people.

In contrast to this group some countries are projected to triple their populations over the next half-century. For example, Ethiopia's current population of 62 million will more than triple, as it climbs to 213 million in 2050. Pakistan's population is projected to go from 148 million to 357 million, surpassing that of the United States before 2050 today to 339 million, giving it more people in 2050 than there were in all of Africa in 1950. From an environmental Vantage point, considering particularly the availability of water and cropland, it is unlikely that the projected population increases for these three countries, and other countries with similar projected gains, will materialize.

As hard as it is to imagine the addition of another 3.3 billion people to the world's population, it is even more difficult to understand the effects of adding such numbers. As we look back over the last half-century, we see that World lumber use more than doubled, paper use increased nearly sixfold, grain consumption nearly tripled, water use tripled, and fossil fuel burning increased some fourfold. The relative contribution of population growth and rising affluence to the growth in demand for various resources varies widely. With lumber use, most of the doubled use is accounted for by population growth. With paper, in contrast, rising affluence is primarily responsible for the growth in use.

One way to understand the consequences of future population growth is to contrast some of the key trend projected for the next half-century with those of as one. For example, we have seen a new fivefold growth in the oceanic fish catch and a doubling in the supply available per person, but biologists now believe we may have 'hit the wall' in oceanic fisheries and that the oceans cannot sustain a catch any larger than today's. Thus people born today are likely to see the catch per person cut in half during their lifetimes.

Grainland per person has been shrinking since midcentury, but the drop projected for the next 50 years means the world will have less grainland per person than India has today. Future population growth is likely to reduce this key number in many societies to the point where they will no longer be enable to feed themselves. Countries such as Ethiopia, India, Nigeria, and Pakistan will see grainland per person shrink by 2050 to less than one-tenth of a hectare (one forth of an acre)—far smaller than a typical suburban building lot in the United States.

Given that at the amount of fresh water produced each year is essentially fixed by nature, the water available, per person has shrunk steadily as a result of population growth, leading to sever water shortages in some areas. Countries now experiencing these shortages include China and India, along with scores of smaller ones. As irrigation water is diverted to industrial and residential uses.

The challenge to governments presented by continuing rapid population growth is not limited to natural resources. It also includes education, housing, and jobs. During the last half-century the world has fallen further and further behind in creating jobs, leading to record levels of unemployment and under employment. Unfortunately over the next 50 years the number of entrants into the job market will be even greater. Few things threaten the political stability of a country as much as growing as growing ranks of unemployed young people.

As noted earlier, the UN population projections cited here are based on exclusively demographic assumptions, which are not related to the population carrying capacity of local eco systems. These projections are purely statistical, based on historical data on fertility, mortality, and average life span and assumptions about future trends.

Based on the analysis in it, I conclude that the medium projection of 9.4 billion people in 2050 which UN demographers consider to be the most problem is unlikely to materialize. Rather the world is more likely to follow a path closer to the low population projection of 7.7 billion by mid-century.

What is less clear is whether we will move to the lower trajectory because countries with rapid pollution growth quickly shift to smaller families or because they fail to do so and the resulting inability to manage threats from disease, spreading hunger, or social disintegration leads to rising death rates.

BIBLIOGRAPHY

1. Agarwala, S.N., *India's Population Problems*, Tata McGraw Hill, Bombay, 1972.

2. Arora, Y.L., 'Infant Mortality and Family Planning', *Journal of Family Welfare,* Vol. XXVI, No.4, June 1980.

3. Agarwala, S.N., 'Social and Cultural Factors Affecting Fertility in India', *Population Review*, Vol. 8, January 1964.

4. Agarwala, S.N., 'Effect of a Raise in Female Marriage Age on Birth Rate in India', Proceedings, World Population Conference, Vol.2, New York: United Nations 1967.

5. Anubharoy, 'Population Control: Doorway to Development', *Southern Economist*, Vol.26, No.20, February, 15, 1988.

6. Bahadur, K.P., *Population Crisis in India*, National Publishing House, 1977.

7. Bhargava, P.K. (1984), 'Age at Marriage and Its Effects on Fertility : A Study of Slum Dwellers in Great Bombay', *The Journal of Family Welfare*, 31(1).

8. Bhargava, P.K., and Saxena, P.C. (1984); *Female Labour Force Participation and Fertility in a Metropolitan City of India,* International Institute *for* Population Sciences, Bombay (Mimeographed).

9. Bhasin, M.G., 'Encouraging One Child Families', *Yojana*, Vol. 28, No.16, September 15, 1984.

10. Bulatao, R.A., and R.D. Lee (eds). 1983. *Determinants of Fertility in Developing Countries*, New York; Academic Press.

11. Berelson, B. and Licherson, J. 1979. 'Government Efforts to Influence Fertility: The Ethical Issues', *Population and Development Review* 5.

12. Bhanogi Rao (1988), 'Fertility Transition—A Study of China and India', *The Economic Times*, Bombay, June 1.

13. Caldwell, J.C. 1980, 'Mass Education as a Determinant of the Timing of Fertility Decline', *Population and Development Review*, (June).

14. Coombs, Clyde H., Holagene C. Coombs, and Gary H. Mc. Clelland 1975, 'Preference Scales for Number and Sex of Children' *Population Studies* 29 (June).

15. Chandrasekhar, S., *Population and Planned Parenthood in India*, George Allen and Union Ltd., London (1955).

16. Caldwell, John C., 'Education as a Factor in Mortality Decline: An Examination of Nigerion Data', *Population Studies*, 33, Vol. 3, 1979.

17. Das Gupta, Monica, 1987, 'Selective Discrimination Against Female Children in Rural Punjab, India', *Population and Development Review*, 13.

18. David, and Warren C. Sanderson, 1987, 'The Emergence of a Two-Child Norm Among American Birth—Controllers', *Population and Development Review* 13, No.1.

19. Ehrlich, P. and Ehrlich, A.H. 1972, p*opulation, Resources, Environment: Issues in Human Ecology,* W.H. Freeman and Co., San Francisco (2nd Ed.)

20. Editorial, 'Facts of India's Population Problem', *Southern Economist*, Vol. 27, No.6, July 15, 1988.

21. Freedman, R. et al. 1959. *Family Planning, Sterlity and Population Growth*, New York: McGraw-Hill.

22. Freedman, R., P.K. Whelpton, and J.Smit 1961. 'Socio-Economic Factors in Religious Differentials in Fertility'. *American Sociological Review* 26, No. 4.

23. Fawcett, J.T. (ed) 1972, *The Satisfactions and Costs of Children: Theories, Concepts, Methods,* East-West Centre, Honolulu.

24. Freedman, Ronald, 1987, 'The Contribution of Social Science Research to Population Policy and Family Planning Programme Effectiveness', *Studies in Family Planning* 18, No.2.

25. Government of India, Ministry of Health and Family Welfare, *Family Welfare Programme Year Book 1986-87,* New Delhi.

26. Gulati, S.S. (1969), 'Impact of Literacy, Urbanisation and Sex Ratio on Age at Marriage in India', *Artha Vijnana* 11.

27. Government of India, *Seventh Five Year Plan,* Planning Commission, 1985-90.

28. Ganguli, B.N., *Population and Development*, S. Chand and Company, Pvt. Ltd. (1973).

29. Goyel, R.P., 'Birth Rate Can be Reduced to a Third by Late Marriage', *Yojana*, August 30, 1964.

30. Hobcraft, J.N., J.W. McDonald, and S.O.Rutstein, 1985.'Demographic Determinants of Infant and Early Child Mortality: A Comparative Analysis', *Population Study* 39, No. 3.

31. Hermudez, Donald J. 1981. 'A Note on Measuring the Independent Impact of Family Planning Programmes on Fertility Declines', *Demography*, 18, No.4.

32. Hohm, C.F., 'Social Security and Fertility: An International Perspective', *Demography*, Vol. 12, 1975.

33. *Indian Institute of Mass Communication, Communication and Family Planning*, Report of an Intensive Family Planning Campaign, New Delhi, 1967.

34. Jauhari, B.M., 'Population Planning in Rural India', *Southern Economist*, Vol. 25, No.4, June 15, 1986.

35. Jain, S.P., 'Indian Fertility—Our Knowledge and Gaps', *The Journal of Family Welfare*, Vol. 10, 1964.

36. Meera Reddy, V., *Family Planning and Economic Development*, (Tirupati, Sri Venkateswara University, 1986).

37. Mueller, E., 'Economic Motives for Family Limitation', *Population Studies*, Vol.1, 27, No.3, 1972.

38. Mauldin, W.P. 1982, 'The Determinants of Fertility Decline in Developing Countries: An Over View of the Available Empirical Evidence', *International Family Planning Perspectives*, 8, No.3 (September).

39. Narain, K.V., 'One Child Families', *The Hindu* (Madras), October 4, 1980.

40. Nag, Moni, 1980, 'How Modernization Can Also Increase Fertility', *Current Anthropology*, 21, No.5.

41. Ogale, S.L., 'The Role of Extension Education, Incentives and Disincentives in Promoting the Small Family Norm', *The Journal of Family Welfare*, Vol. 15, March 1969.

42. Proffenberger, Thomas, 1969, *Husband-Wife Communication and Motivational Aspect of Population Control in an Indian Village*, New Delhi, Central Family Planning Institute.

43. Preston, Samuel H. (ed), 1978. *The Effects of Infant and Child Mortality Upon Fertility*, New York, Academic Press.

Index